SUBLIMATION COOKBOOK

Handy one-page "recipes" for
150+ popular sublimation projects

BY
JENNIFERMAKER

ABOUT THIS COOKBOOK

In this cookbook, you will find **recipes for sublimating everything I could think of**, as well as all the information you need on the equipment, times, temperatures, pressures, and other details to create beautiful sublimation projects. This is essentially your personal pre-filled sublimation notebook with all the information others may spend years or decades collecting — you can even add your own notes and tips as you go along!

Are you new to sublimation? Sublimation is a crafting process that allows you to take a detailed image and apply it to items made of polyester or with sublimation-friendly coatings. The ink from the sublimation print then infuses with the material's surface when high heat is applied. The sublimation process requires you to use specific equipment and supplies, such as special sublimation ink, sublimation paper, and a heat source. You will also need to apply the sublimation transfer to a sublimation-specific item, called a blank, for the best results.

Hello, I'm Jennifer!

To learn more about the process of sublimation, check out my **beginner-friendly guide** over at jennifermaker.com/sublimation-for-beginners. To learn about the supplies and tools I recommend, visit jennifermaker.com/sublimation-supplies.

If you have any **questions** about this cookbook, please ask in my Sublimation Made Easy by JenniferMaker group at jennifermaker.com/sublimationgroup or email at vip@jennifermaker.com.

Happy sublimating,

Jennifer

Version 1.09 - Print Edition - November 2023 • Copyright 2023 by JenniferMaker Creative Living. • ISBN 978-1-64737-004-6

COOKBOOK PAGES

SUBLIMATION EQUIPMENT

Throughout this sublimation cookbook, you will use various equipment to complete the recipes. Below is a list of the equipment, a brief description of each item, and a few of my favorite brands to use. You are welcome to use the equipment that you have on hand. Please note that you will only need some of the equipment listed to complete any single recipe. You can review more information on our recommended supplies at jennifermaker.com/sublimation-supplies.

EQUIPMENT USED
- ☐ Heat source
  - ☐ Flat heat press
  - ☐ Tumbler or mug press
  - ☐ Convection oven or air fryer
- ☐ Pressing pad
- ☐ Pillow or foam
- ☐ Heat-resistant gloves
- ☐ Microfiber cloth
- ☐ Lint roller
- ☐ Ruler or fabric measuring tape
- ☐ Scissors
- ☐ Weeding tool
- ☐ Pen or Pencil
- ☐ Rubbing alcohol
- ☐ Cardboard

OPTIONAL EQUIPMENT USED
- ☐ Cutting machine
- ☐ Heat gun
- ☐ Shrink wrap
- ☐ Silicone bands
- ☐ Silicone flask wrap
- ☐ Silicone wrap

NOTE ON HEAT SOURCES
You will see several heat sources listed throughout this cookbook, including a traditional heat press, Cricut AutoPress, Cricut EasyPress, Cricut MiniPress, Cricut Mug Press, traditional tumbler press, convection oven, and air fryer. Use what is appropriate for the sublimation blank and the recipe.

Flat Heat Press
The flat heat press provides heat to pre-press and sublimate on blanks with flat surfaces. I like to use the Cricut AutoPress and EasyPress.

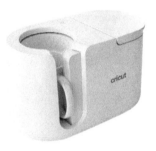

Mug Press
The mug press is used primarily to heat the sublimation transfer to a mug and other glassware. I like to use the Cricut Mug Press.

Tumbler Heat Press
The tumbler press is used primarily for drinkware. The press should fit snuggly against the drinkware to heat evenly during sublimation.

Convection Oven
A countertop model with removable racks will work best. Convection ovens are used to heat items that will not work with a flat press.

Air Fryer
An 8 qt. or larger air fryer will work best for a variety of blanks. An air fryer can be used as an alternative heat source for sublimating.

IMPORTANT NOTE:
Once you use a convection oven or an air fryer for sublimation, it is unsafe to use for cooking food due to the process that the ink goes through when sublimating.

Pressing Pad
A pressing pad will be used to support even pressure when pressing your blanks.

Pressing Pillow or Foam
The pressing pillow or foam will go inside your blanks. This is used when you have zippers or uneven pressing areas and will help ensure you have an even pressing surface.

Heat-Resistant Gloves
Any gloves designed to protect your hands from heat will be fine. It is important to use heat-resistant gloves when removing items from the pressing area.

Microfiber Cloth
This item can be purchased from any retail store. This will be used to remove dust and debris from your sublimation blanks.

Lint Roller
Use a lint roller with disposable sticky sheets to help remove dirt, dust, and debris from your sublimation blanks.

Ruler or Measuring Tape
Any ruler or measuring tape can be used to measure the blanks and the transfer sheet images.

Scissors
Any scissors used for cutting paper will be fine. These will be used to cut the sublimation transfer sheet and other items.

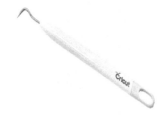

Weeding Tool
The weeding tool can be helpful when removing small pieces of transfer prints, tape, and protective coatings on blanks. Use caution so that you do not scratch your blank.

Fan
It is very important to use a fan and have good ventilation, like an open window, when sublimating because the fumes can be noxious.

OPTIONAL EQUIPMENT:

Other items
Cardboard, rubbing alcohol, and a pen or pencil can be regular household items.

Cutting Machine
Using the print-then-cut feature, you can use the cutting machine to cut out your sublimation blanks. I love my Cricuts!

Silicone Bands
There are a variety of silicone bands available. These bands are used to secure the transfer print and wrap to tumblers, mugs, and drinkware.

Shrink Wrap
Use clear or white shrink wrap. You can find shrink wrap bags for drinkware. Specialized silicone wraps are also interchangeable with shrink wrap.

Heat Gun
The heat gun is an optional heat source for sublimation blanks that do not fit in the traditional heat press, as well as for recipes that use shrink wrap.

For more information on our recommended equipment, supplies, and materials, please visit: jennifermaker.com/ sublimation-supplies/

INGREDIENTS: THE BASICS

What do you need for sublimation? The essential ingredients are some clean blowout paper, heat-resistant tape, and a sublimation transfer sheet. In the following pages, you will find information on each of these items and the common blanks that will be covered in the cookbook.

BLANKS: A blank is an item you will sublimate your design on. Blanks that are specifically designed to accept sublimation ink come with a special coating already applied or are made with a high percentage of polyester. Blanks can be stainless steel, ceramic, MDF & HDF, glass, slate, aluminum, acrylic & plastic, wood, vinyl, paper, cardboard, neoprene, and more.

NON-SUBLIMATION BLANKS: Blanks that are not designed to accept sublimation ink can still be used with the help of an extra ingredient. You can use clear Heat Transfer Vinyl (HTV), white glitter HTV, holographic HTV, glow-in-the-dark HTV, EasySubli, DTV, DTF, thermal lamination sheets, and sublimation spray to help create a surface that you can sublimate onto.

BLOWOUT PAPER: Blowout paper is used to create a barrier between your blank and your heat source, to keep sublimation ink from getting anywhere except on the blank, and to put in between layers of a blank, i.e. inside a shirt. I recommend that you use white cardstock and/or white uncoated butcher paper so there is no risk of ink from the paper transferring to your blank, pressing pad, or the platen of your heat press.

HEAT-RESISTANT TAPE: Heat-resistant tape keeps your sublimation transfer firmly secured to your blank during the pressing process, which helps eliminate blurring and ghosting. It comes in a few colors, but some are meant for something other than sublimation because they can stain your blank. I prefer the Cricut brand, which is blue.

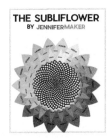

SUBLIMATION TRANSFER (PRINT/SHEET): This is the design or image that you want to transfer to your blank. It can be printed on sublimation paper using sublimation ink, cut out from Infusible Ink, or applied to sublimation or laser copy paper using sublimation pens, markers, paint, or stamps and stamp pads. Remember that often this image must be mirrored prior to printing to show up correctly on the finished blank.

INGREDIENTS: COMMON BLANKS

 **POLYESTER:** The fabric blank must be at least 65% polyester, but the higher the polyester percentage, the more vibrant your sublimation image will be. Polyester blanks are usually soft and flexible. These blanks typically require a flat heat press, except hats.

 **STAINLESS STEEL:** Stainless steel blanks often come as drinkware, like tumblers and camping mugs. The outside walls of these blanks must be coated for sublimation by the manufacturer. These blanks need tumbler or mug presses, a convection oven, or an air fryer.

 **CERAMIC:** Ceramic blanks can be flat or three-dimensional. Flat blanks, such as ornaments and tiles, need a flat heat press. Flat ceramic blanks may be coated on one or both sides, and three-dimensional blanks are coated only on the outside wall. Three-dimensional blanks, such as mugs or bowls, will require a mug press, convection oven, or air fryer.

 **MDF & HDF:** MDF (medium-density fiberboard) and HDF (high-density fiberboard) blanks are flat and come in many shapes and sizes, from tags and ornaments to photo frames and puzzles. These may be coated for sublimation on one or both sides. These blanks should be pressed using a flat heat press.

 **GLASS:** Glass blanks can be flat or three-dimensional, and must be heat resistant. Flat glass blanks, such as ornaments, tiles, and cutting boards, should be pressed using a flat heat press. Most glass blanks are only coated for sublimation on one side. Three-dimensional glass blanks, such as drinkware, will require a tumbler or mug press, convection oven, or air fryer.

INGREDIENTS: COMMON BLANKS

SLATE: Slate rock blanks come in multiple shapes and sizes and are often used as plaques, awards, and photos. They are only coated white for sublimation on one side and should be pressed with a flat heat press.

ALUMINUM: Aluminum blanks, such as license plates, photo panels, and dog tags, are often flat. They may be coated for sublimation on one or both sides. These blanks require a flat heat press.

ACRYLIC & PLASTIC: Acrylic, plastic, and FRP (fiber-reinforced plastic) blanks range from keychains and ornaments to faux leather and frisbees. These blanks may be coated for sublimation on one or both sides and require a flat heat press.

WOOD: Wood blanks, such as plaques, wall signs, and charcuterie boards, are usually flat and may be coated for sublimation on one or both sides. These blanks require a flat heat press.

VINYL, PAPER, & CARDBOARD: Vinyl, paper, and cardboard blanks may or may not be specially coated for sublimation. These blanks require a flat heat press.

NEOPRENE: Neoprene is a synthetic rubber and is often seen in the form of mousepads, lunch bags, and laptop sleeves. These blanks must be coated for sublimation and require a flat heat press.

PRESSURES AND TEMPERATURES

The sublimation process requires determining the time, pressures, and temperature for each project. The combination of these three essential steps is what will make the recipes in this cookbook possible. Please review the information below to help you understand the importance of pressure and temperatures. This page also contains key information about two common sublimating issues: ghosting and improper taping.

PRESSURE

Pressure is the amount of resistance applied to your blank from the heat press. For an Autopress, this is done automatically by the machine. You will need to apply this pressure level with your hand for hand-held presses. Throughout the cookbook, you will see three pressure settings: 30 psi (light), 40 psi (medium), and 50 psi (heavy). A sublimation transfer will most often require medium pressure or 40 psi. The correct amount of pressure allows the heat to distribute evenly across the blank. If your pressure is too high, it can cause uneven ink saturation across your product. If it is too low, the colors will not be as vibrant as the original design.

TEMPERATURE

Temperature refers to the temperature setting on your heat press, convection oven, or air fryer. The correct temperature is very important to creating an adequately sublimated product. A temperature setting that is too high can cause discoloration or ghosting or even melt or warp the blank. Some of the materials with a plastic or acrylic component have a lower heat requirement due to the melting point of the materials. A temperature setting that is too low will not allow the ink to saturate the blank material, resulting in little or no ink transfer.

HOW THE PRESSURE AND TEMPERATURE SETTINGS APPEAR IN THE RECIPES

Near the bottom of each recipe, there is a chart that outlines the typical temperature, pressure, and time requirements for pressing the sublimation blank. Please note that these times and temperatures can vary with your specific materials and the type of press being used, so always check the instructions that come with your blanks. Additional details about the pre-pressing temperatures and times will be within the recipe directions.

Please note that when mentioning the EasyPress in our heat guide we are referring to the EasyPress 2 and 3. The original EasyPresswill work for some sublimation projects that require lower temps, but not others, like ceramic. Increasing the time does not make a difference there.

Below is an example of the pressing requirements chart on every recipe page. Note that there is a column for you to record your preferred settings.

your favorite settings

Traditional Heat Press	AutoPress	EasyPress	Mini Press	
385°F / 196°C	400°F / 204°C	385°F / 196°C	High	
45-60 seconds	45 seconds	40 seconds	70 seconds	
40 psi (light/medium)	Auto pressure	Light pressure	Light pressure	

COMMON ISSUES WITH SUBLIMATION

GHOSTING
Ghosting, or blurring, is a common challenge with sublimation. Ghosting most often occurs when there is a shift in your sublimation print during the pressing process. This typically happens when you apply or remove the heat press while the ink is in the sublimation process but has yet to dry. Ghosting can also occur when the temperature is set too high, or the blank is cooked for too long.

IMPROPER TAPING
Heat-resistant tape is designed to help secure your sublimation transfer on your sublimation blank during the sublimation process. This will help eliminate any ghosting. Taping all edges of the sublimation transfer to the blank will yield the best results. Heat-resistant tape can withstand temperatures up to 425°F / 218°C.

PRINTING

Creating sublimation transfers requires specific printers, ink, and settings. On this page, you will find information on what to use to get the best quality sublimation transfer prints. For more information on the different sublimation printers check out jennifermaker.com/best-sublimation-printer/

RECOMMENDED PRINTERS

Two types of printers can be used for sublimation. Here are my recommendations:
• Purpose-built sublimation printers: Sawgrass SG500 or SG1000, Epson F170 or F570
• Converted sublimation printers: Epson Ecotank (any model)

SUBLIMATION INK

You must use sublimation ink in your printer to create sublimatable designs. Once you use a specific brand of sublimation ink in your printer, do not use any other brand to refill it. Inkjet ink will not work for the sublimation process.

ICC PROFILES

An ICC profile is a specific set of color information for a printer, which helps create true and vibrant colors when an image is printed. You can find ICC profiles for many printers and ink brands online.

BEST SETTINGS

To get the best results, choose "Presentation Paper Matte" for your paper type. Even if your printer says the paper is a mismatch, you can still use this setting. Always choose the highest print quality available, which is usually "Highest" or "Best."

WHERE TO PRINT YOUR DESIGNS FROM

You can choose to print your sublimation design from a variety of programs. Many people choose to print from Google Docs, Microsoft Word, Inkscape, Photoshop, and Cricut Design Space using Print then Cut (you don't have to have a Cricut to do this). However, if you create your design on Canva, you must download it and print from one of these, as you cannot print directly from Canva.

PRINTING

• Print on sublimation paper. Sublimation paper comes in a few different weights or thicknesses. The thicker the paper, the more ink it can hold, meaning the printed design will be more vibrant.
• Don't judge your print before you press it. Sublimation prints don't reflect the true colors on paper and will instead appear washed out or pale. You need to press your design and transfer the colors to your blank before you can truly see what it looks like.
• If using a converted printer, be sure to print something weekly to prevent the ink from drying out.

FREE SUBLIMATION DESIGNS

Are you still trying to figure out what you want to print for your sublimation projects? View over 100 designs free for you to use at jennifermaker.com/free-sublimation-designs/

OTHER FORMS OF SUBLIMATION INK

Although sublimation ink is most often used in a printer, it comes in several forms.

INFUSIBLE INK SHEETS

Cricut Infusible Ink sheets come in a variety of patterns and colors and can be used with a cutting machine.

SUBLIMATION/INFUSIBLE INK PENS & MARKERS

Use sublimation pens and markers to draw on sublimation paper or laser copy paper, then transfer the design to your blank.

SUBLIMATION PAINT

Use sublimation paint and a paintbrush to paint on thick paper, such as white cardstock or watercolor paper. Then, transfer the design to your blank.

SUBLIMATION STAMP PADS

Sublimation stamp pads work with any stamps. Use these to stamp outlines on paper, then fill them in with sublimation pens or markers before transferring the design to your blank.

CUTTING YOUR SUBLIMATION PRINTS

It is important to make sure that your sublimation transfer print is correctly sized to fit on a sublimation blank in order to help minimize ghosting. There are three main ways to cut your sublimation prints to fit a sublimation bank.

TRIM CLOSE TO INK

Use this method for any sublimation transfer that is smaller than the surface of your sublimation blank.

Use scissors or a paper trimmer to cut away as much excess sublimation paper as possible, leaving very little white paper (less than a quarter inch) around the edges of the design.

FEATHER THE EDGES

Use this method for polyester blanks, which are often fluffy, fuzzy, soft, and flexible.

Tear the edges around the sublimation transfer at an angle. This will eliminate some of the thickness of the paper, which will help minimize the appearance of paper lines on your blank.

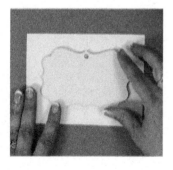

LEAVE EXTRA SPACE

Use this method for any sublimation transfer that will cover the entire surface of your sublimation blank.

Use scissors to trim most of the excess sublimation paper away, but be sure to leave at least a quarter inch (or more) around the edges of the design.

CHAPTER 1
POLYESTER

T-SHIRTS 65–100% POLYESTER

ALSO: Hoodies, tanks, long-sleeved shirts, polos, infant bodysuits, bleached shirts, and other garments

This popular recipe calls for T-shirts of any style made of 65-100% polyester knit. Can be blended with cotton, rayon, spandex, and other fibers. White and light colors work best.

INGREDIENTS

☐ White or light T-shirt of at least 65% polyester knit (brands such as Cricut, Gildan, Hanes)
☐ Blowout paper (two sheets)
☐ Heat-resistant tape
☐ Sublimation transfer

EQUIPMENT

☐ Lint roller
☐ Flat heat source such as a heat press
☐ (Optional) T-shirt ruler for placement help
☐ (Optional) Pillow or foam for shirts with buttons, seams, zippers, or pockets

PREPARATION

Start with a new shirt for the best results. No need to pre-wash, but if you do, avoid fabric softener.

Pre-heat your flat heat press to the temperature shown in chart below.

Tear or very closely trim the edges of your printed sublimation transfer to minimize the appearance of paper lines on your finished shirt. (Not necessary when using transfer sheets like Infusible Ink.) Double check your image to make sure it is correctly mirrored if needed.

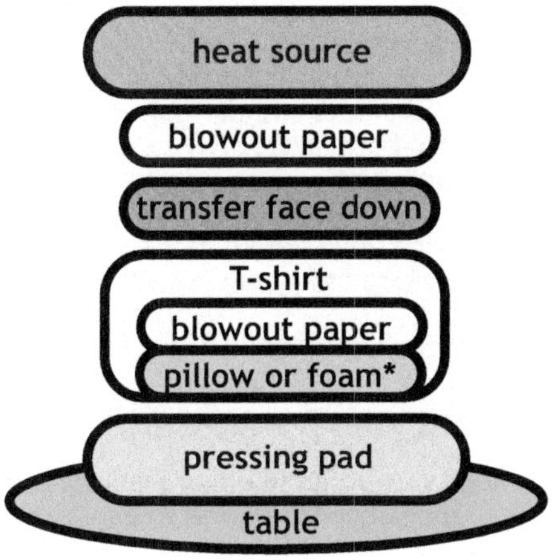

Lint roll your shirt to remove any dust or debris.

Fold shirt in half lengthwise so both sides match up, then press for 10 seconds — this both pre-heats the shirt to remove moisture and gives you a straight vertical crease for alignment.

Unfold shirt and **slide a piece of blowout paper inside your shirt** (I recommend white cardstock) to keep the sublimation ink from bleeding into the other side of the shirt. Optionally, you can also place a pressing pillow under the paper inside your shirt — this is helpful if you have any raised areas on your shirt (button, seam, zipper, pocket, etc.) which may make it hard to press down evenly.

Crease your sublimation transfer vertically at the top and bottom (but not where there is ink) and **align creases** with vertical creases in your shirt.

Tape all four edges of your design face down on your shirt about two inches below the collar seam (crew neck) or one inch below the seam (V-neck or children's sizes). A T-shirt ruler can help more with placement. Place a sheet of blowout paper on top. Press according to the chart below.

heat source
blowout paper
transfer face down
T-shirt
blowout paper
pillow or foam*
pressing pad
table

* optional

COOK TIMES

Here are typical times you can use as a starting point. Always check the manufacturer's instructions for time and temperature, when available.

your favorite settings

Traditional Heat Press	AutoPress	Easy Press	Mini Press	
385°F / 196°C	400°F / 204°C	385°F / 196°C	High	
45-60 seconds	45 seconds	40 seconds	70 seconds	
40 psi (light/medium)	Auto pressure	Light pressure	Light pressure	

TIPS & TRICKS

✗ Don't remove your sublimation transfer sheet for at least 10 seconds so it can cool down without ghosting.
✓ For a tutorial on how to sublimate a T-Shirt check out jennifermaker.com/sublimation-t-shirt/
✓ If you're pressing a sublimation design over seams, medium to firm pressure works better.
✓ After Care: Wash inside out in cold water with mild detergent, no bleach, no fabric softener, tumble dry low.

TIE-DYE SHIRTS
65–100% POLYESTER

Create a tie-dye effect using this method. White and light colored shirts work best. This recipe uses a circular pattern, but you can use several other patterns to get unique effects.

INGREDIENTS

☐ White or light T-shirt of at least 65% polyester knit (brands such as Cricut, Gildan, Hanes)
☐ Blowout paper (two sheets)
☐ Heat-resistant tape
☐ Sublimation transfer

EQUIPMENT

☐ Lint roller
☐ Flat heat source such as a heat press
☐ (Optional) T-shirt ruler for placement help

PREPARATION

Start with a new shirt for the best results. No need to pre-wash, but if you do, avoid fabric softener.

Pre-heat your flat heat press to the temperature shown in chart below.

Use a lint roller to clean the shirt.

Place a piece of blowout paper on the pressing area. Lay your t-shirt **face up** on top.

To create a circular pattern, pinch the center of the shirt, making sure to grab both layers. **Twist counter-clockwise** until the shirt eventually looks like a circle. Keep your twists tight and arrange them as you go.

Place your sublimation transfer face down on top of the shirt and secure it in place using heat-resistant tape.

Place a sheet of blowout paper on top.

Press according to the chart below. Remove the transfer while still warm.

If you would like more color, repeat the process, but twist so that the shirt appears mostly white when viewed from the top.

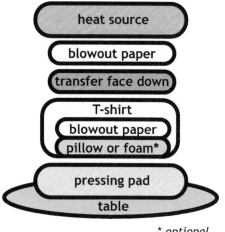

heat source

blowout paper

transfer face down

T-shirt

blowout paper

pillow or foam*

pressing pad

table

optional

COOK TIMES

Here are typical times you can use as a starting point. Always check the manufacturer's instructions for time and temperature, when available.

your favorite settings

Traditional Heat Press	AutoPress	Easy Press	Mini Press	
385°F / 196°C	385°F / 196°C	385°F / 196°C	High	
45-60 seconds	60 seconds	60 seconds	70 seconds	
40 psi (light/medium)	Auto pressure	Medium pressure	Medium pressure	

TIPS & TRICKS

✗ Don't remove your sublimation transfer sheet for at least 10 seconds so it can cool down without ghosting.
✓ When securing the sublimation transfer down, tape it to the blowout paper rather than the shirt. This will help create a neat little package to help contain the shirt.
✓ If you're pressing a sublimation design over seams, medium to firm pressure works better.
✓ For a tutorial on how to sublimate a tie-dye shirt in other folding and twisting patterns, check out jennifermaker. com/how-to-make-a-cool-tie-dye-shirt/
✓ After Care: Wash inside out in cold water with mild detergent, no bleach, no fabric softener, tumble dry low.

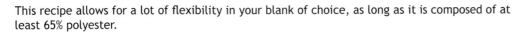

HATS POLYESTER

ALSO: Ballcaps, visors, bucket hats

This recipe allows for a lot of flexibility in your blank of choice, as long as it is composed of at least 65% polyester.

INGREDIENTS
☐ Hat (of at least 65% polyester)
☐ Butcher paper (one sheet)
☐ Heat-resistant tape
☐ Sublimation transfer (print/sheet)

EQUIPMENT
☐ Lint roller
☐ Hat press or mini press
☐ Hat press form

PREPARATION

Start with a new hat for the best results. No need to pre-wash, but if you do, avoid fabric softener.

Pre-heat your hat press to the temperature shown in the chart below.

Very closely trim the edges of your sublimation transfer to minimize the appearance of paper lines on the finished hat.

Insert hat form into the inside of your hat if using the Cricut hat press or mini press. Make sure it is secure and fits snugly. If using a traditional hat press, lay the hat on the press so the back of the hat is hanging down and the front is against the platen.

Use the lint roller on the surface of the hat to remove any fuzz or debris.

Place a piece of butcher paper over the surface of your hat. **Place the hat press** over the butcher paper and pre-heat your hat for 5 seconds. **Remove the butcher paper.**

Tape all edges of your sublimation transfer face down on your hat. **Cover it with a piece of butcher paper.**

Press according to the chart below. Pull the transfer sheet while still warm.

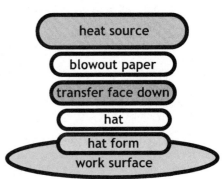
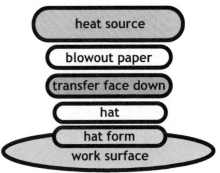

heat source
blowout paper
transfer face down
hat
hat form
work surface

COOK TIMES
Here are typical times you can use as a starting point. Always check the manufacturer's instructions for time and temperature, when available.

your favorite settings

Traditional Hat Press	Cricut Hat Press	Mini Press	
350°F / 176°C	High	High	
60 seconds	90 seconds	90 seconds	
30 psi (light pressure)	Light pressure	Medium pressure	

TIPS & TRICKS
✓ Remember to mirror the design before printing your sublimation transfer.
✓ For a hat press tutorial check out jennifermaker.com/cricut-hat-press/
✗ Don't remove your sublimation transfer sheet for at least 10 seconds so it can cool down without ghosting.
✓ If your sublimation design is mostly black, you may want to add an extra 10-20 seconds.
✓ Make sure that your hat is securely fitted over your press form. A hat that is too loose may result in ghosting.
✓ After Care: Hand wash only. Do not bleach. Line dry.

TOTE BAGS POLYESTER

ALSO: Pouches, makeup bags, backpacks

Tote bags at least 65% polyester will make a perfect recipe for carrying your things.

INGREDIENTS
☐ Tote bag (of at least 65% polyester)
☐ Blowout paper (two sheets)
☐ Heat-resistant tape
☐ Sublimation transfer (print/sheet)

EQUIPMENT
☐ Lint roller
☐ Flat heat source such as a heat press
☐ (Optional) Ruler or fabric tape measure for placement help
☐ (Optional) Pillow or form for totes with seams, zippers, or pockets

PREPARATION

Start with a new tote bag for the best results. No need to pre-wash, but if you do, avoid fabric softener.

Pre-heat your flat heat press to the temperature shown in the chart below.

Very closely trim the edges of your sublimation transfer to minimize the appearance of paper lines on your finished tote bag.

Use the lint roller to remove any extra pieces of fiber from your tote bag.

Press the tote bag with your heat press for 5 seconds to pre-heat it and remove any moisture.

Place a piece of blowout paper (I recommend white cardstock or butcher paper) inside the tote bag to keep the sublimation ink from bleeding into the other side of the tote bag. Optionally, you can also place a pressing pillow under the paper inside your tote bag.

Using heat resistant tape, secure all edges of your sublimation transfer face down on your tote bag. A ruler may help with placement.

Place a piece of blowout paper (I recommend white cardstock or butcher paper) on your pressing pad, then lay the tote bag on top of the blowout paper. **Cover with another sheet of blowout paper.**

Press according to the chart below. Pull the transfer sheet while still warm.

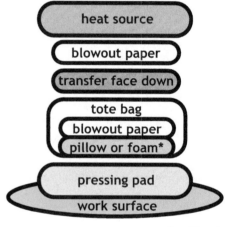

heat source
blowout paper
transfer face down
tote bag
blowout paper
pillow or foam*
pressing pad
work surface

* optional

COOK TIMES
Here are typical times you can use as a starting point. Always check the manufacturer's instructions for time and temperature, when available.

your favorite settings

Traditional Heat Press	AutoPress	EasyPress	Mini Press	
400°F / 204°C	385°F / 195°C	385°F / 195°C	High	
45 seconds	50 seconds	40 seconds	75 seconds	
40 psi (medium pressure)	Auto pressure	Firm pressure	Firm pressure	

TIPS & TRICKS
✓ Remember to mirror the design before printing your sublimation transfer.
✗ Don't remove your sublimation transfer sheet for at least 10 seconds so it can cool down without ghosting.
✗ Don't press over any zippers or snaps.
✓ If you're pressing a sublimation design over seams, medium to firm pressure works better.
✗ Unless you are specifically sublimating the handles of the tote bag, keep them out of the way of the heat press.
✓ If sublimating a backpack, be sure to use a pillow or form inside.

MICROFIBER TOWELS
POLYESTER
ALSO: Microfiber pillowcases

Microfiber towels made of at least 65% polyester will make great decorative additions to your kitchen or bathroom. Waffle-weave towels are readily available and add texture.

INGREDIENTS
☐ Microfiber towel (at least 65% polyester)
☐ Blowout paper (two sheets)
☐ Heat-resistant tape
☐ Sublimation transfer (print/sheet)

EQUIPMENT
☐ Lint roller
☐ Flat heat source such as a heat press
☐ (Optional) Ruler or fabric tape measure for placement help

PREPARATION

Start with a new towel for the best results. No need to pre-wash, but if you do, avoid fabric softener.

Pre-heat your flat heat press to the temperature shown in chart below.

Very closely trim the edges of your sublimation transfer to minimize the appearance of paper lines on your finished microfiber towel.

Use the lint roller to remove any extra pieces of fiber in the area you want to press.

Run your hand over the area to make the fibers go in the same direction.

Press the towel with your heat press for 5 seconds to pre-heat it and remove any moisture.

Using heat-resistant tape, secure all edges of your sublimation transfer face down on your microfiber towel. A ruler may help with placement.

Place a piece of blowout paper (I recommend white cardstock or butcher paper) on your pressing pad, then lay the towel on top of the blowout paper. **Cover with another sheet of blowout paper.**

Press according to the chart below. Pull the transfer sheet while still warm.

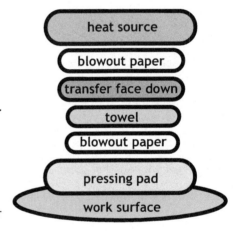

heat source
blowout paper
transfer face down
towel
blowout paper
pressing pad
work surface

COOK TIMES
Here are typical times you can use as a starting point. Always check the manufacturer's instructions for time and temperature, when available.

your favorite settings

Traditional Heat Press	AutoPress	EasyPress	Mini Press	
385°F / 196°C	400°F / 204°C	375°F / 190°C	High	
45 seconds	45 seconds	60 seconds	70 seconds	
40 psi (medium pressure)	Auto pressure	Light pressure	Light pressure	

TIPS & TRICKS
✓ Remember to mirror the design before printing your sublimation transfer.
✗ Don't remove your sublimation transfer sheet for at least 10 seconds so it can cool down without ghosting.
✓ For a tutorial check out jennifermaker.com/Dollar-Tree-Sublimation-Ideas/
✗ Flour sack towels, though popular, are usually 100% cotton. Sublimated ink will not infuse into the blank.
✓ After Care: Washing after will help the towel fibers return to a normal, fluffy state.

APRONS POLYESTER

This recipe allows you to create a personalized apron for the baker or chef in your life. Choose an apron with or without pockets.

INGREDIENTS
☐ Apron (of at least 65% polyester)
☐ Blowout paper (two sheets)
☐ Heat-resistant tape
☐ Sublimation transfer (print/sheet)

EQUIPMENT
☐ Lint roller
☐ Flat heat source such as a heat press
☐ (Optional) Ruler or fabric tape measure for placement help
☐ (Optional) Pillow or form for apron seams or pockets

PREPARATION

Start with a new apron for the best results. No need to pre-wash, but if you do, avoid fabric softener.

Pre-heat your flat heat press to the temperature shown in the chart below.

Tear or very closely trim the edges of your sublimation transfer to minimize the appearance of paper lines on your finished apron.

Use the lint roller to remove any extra pieces of fiber in the area you want to press.

Press the apron with your heat press for 5 seconds to pre-heat it and remove any moisture.

Using heat-resistant tape, secure all edges of your sublimation transfer face down on your apron. A ruler can help with placement.

Place a piece of blowout paper (I recommend white cardstock or butcher paper) on your pressing pad, then lay the apron on top of the blowout paper. **Cover with another sheet of blowout paper.**

Press according to the chart below. Pull the transfer sheet while still warm.

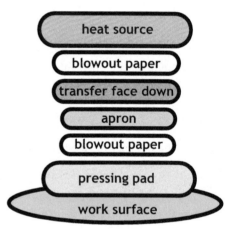

heat source
blowout paper
transfer face down
apron
blowout paper
pressing pad
work surface

COOK TIMES
Here are typical times you can use as a starting point. Always check the manufacturer's instructions for time and temperature, when available.

your favorite settings

Traditional Heat Press	AutoPress	EasyPress	Mini Press	
400°F/ 204°C	385°F / 195°C	385°F / 195°C	High	
60 seconds	50 seconds	40 seconds	75 seconds	
40 psi (medium pressure)	Auto pressure	Firm pressure	Firm pressure	

TIPS & TRICKS
✓ Remember to mirror the design before printing your sublimation transfer.
✗ Don't remove your sublimation transfer sheet for at least 10 seconds so it can cool down without ghosting.
✓ If your sublimation design is mostly black, you may want to add an extra 10-20 seconds.
✓ If you're pressing a sublimation design over seams, medium to firm pressure works better.
✗ Make sure the neck ties and apron strings are out of the way of the heat press.
✓ Optionally, if sublimating on the apron pocket, use a pillow or form inside due to the seams.
✓ After Care: Wash in cold water with mild detergent, no bleach, no fabric softener, and tumble dry low.

BLANKETS POLYESTER FLEECE

ALSO: Fleece jackets, fleece baby bibs, fleece burp cloths

Fleece is a fluffy fabric usually made of polyester, and is a popular material choice for wearables and blankets.

INGREDIENTS
☐ Fleece blanket (of at least 65% polyester)
☐ Blowout paper (two sheets)
☐ Heat-resistant tape
☐ Sublimation transfer (print/sheet)

EQUIPMENT
☐ Lint roller
☐ Flat heat source such as a heat press
☐ (Optional) Ruler or fabric tape measure for placement help

PREPARATION

Start with a new blanket for the best results. No need to pre-wash, but if you do, avoid fabric softener.

Pre-heat your flat heat press to the temperature shown in the chart below.

Very closely tear the edges of your sublimation transfer to minimize the appearance of paper lines on your finished blanket.

Use the lint roller to remove any extra pieces of fiber or fluff in the area you want to press.

Run your hand over the area to make the fibers go in the same direction.

Press the blanket with your heat press for 5 seconds to pre-heat it and remove any moisture.

Using heat-resistant tape, secure all edges of your sublimation transfer face down on your blanket. A ruler may help with placement.

Place a piece of blowout paper (I recommend white cardstock or butcher paper) on your pressing pad, then lay the blanket on top of the blowout paper. **Cover with another sheet of blowout paper.**

Press according to the chart below. Pull the transfer sheet while still warm.

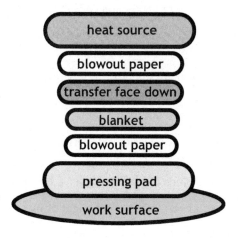

heat source
blowout paper
transfer face down
blanket
blowout paper
pressing pad
work surface

COOK TIMES
Here are typical times you can use as a starting point. Always check the manufacturer's instructions for time and temperature, when available.

your favorite settings

Traditional Heat Press	AutoPress	EasyPress	Mini Press	
385°F / 196°C	350°F /176°C	385°F / 196°C	High	
70 seconds	60 seconds	60-70 seconds	70 seconds	
30 psi (light pressure)	Auto pressure	Light pressure	Light pressure	

TIPS & TRICKS
✓ Remember to mirror the design before printing your sublimation transfer.
✓ If your sublimation design is mostly black, you may want to add an extra 10-20 seconds.
✓ After Care: Washing after will help the blanket fibers return to a normal, fluffy state.
✓ You CAN sublimate on a pastel-colored blanket if you make your design more saturated. Light colors will not show up well on a colored blanket, and white areas of your design will instead be the color of your blanket.
✓ For a tutorial check out jennifermaker.com/Dollar-Tree-Sublimation-Ideas/

PLUSHIES POLYESTER

Customize polyester plushies and other stuffed huggables with this recipe. These can be used as birth announcements, holiday and birthday gifts, and more.

INGREDIENTS

☐ Plushie (of at least 65% polyester)
☐ Blowout paper (two sheets)
☐ Heat-resistant tape
☐ Sublimation transfer (print/sheet)

EQUIPMENT

☐ Lint roller
☐ Flat heat source such as a heat press
☐ (Optional) Ruler or fabric tape measure for placement help

PREPARATION

Start with a new plushie for the best results. No need to pre-wash, but if you do, avoid fabric softener.

Pre-heat your flat heat press to the temperature shown in the chart below.

Very closely tear the edges of your sublimation transfer to minimize the appearance of paper lines on your finished plushie.

Use the lint roller to remove any extra pieces of fiber or fluff in the area you want to press.

Run your hand over the area to make the fibers go in the same direction.

Press the plushie with your heat press for 5 seconds to pre-heat it and remove any moisture.

Tape all four edges of your design face down on your plushie. A ruler may help with placement.

Place a piece of blowout paper (I recommend white cardstock or butcher paper) on your pressing pad, then lay the plushie on top of the blowout paper. **Cover with another sheet of blowout paper.**

Press according to the chart below. Pull the transfer sheet while still warm.

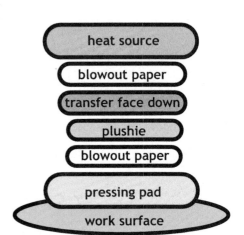

heat source
blowout paper
transfer face down
plushie
blowout paper
pressing pad
work surface

COOK TIMES

Here are typical times you can use as a starting point. Always check the manufacturer's instructions for time and temperature, when available.

your favorite settings

Traditional Heat Press	AutoPress	EasyPress	Mini Press	
385°F / 196°C	385°F / 196°C	385°F / 196°C	High	
70 seconds	60 seconds	60-70 seconds	70 seconds	
50 psi (heavy pressure)	Auto pressure	Heavy pressure	Heavy pressure	

TIPS & TRICKS

✓ Remember to mirror the design before printing your sublimation transfer.
✓ Make sure you are using enough pressure to flatten the plushie down as much as possible. If the plushie is not flattened enough, it may result in ghosting.
✓ It can be tricky to apply pressure to the appropriate area of the plushie. If sublimating on the tummy section, let the head hang outside of the heat press. If sublimating floppy ears, try to place only the ears in the heat press.
✓ You CAN sublimate on a pastel-colored plushie if you keep your design to darker and more saturated colors.

OVEN MITTS POLYESTER

ALSO: Pot holders

Customize sublimatable polyester oven mitts with this recipe. Keep them for yourself, or tie with a wooden spoon and cookie mix as a gift.

INGREDIENTS
☐ Polyester oven mitt (of at least 65% polyester)
☐ Blowout paper (three sheets)
☐ Heat-resistant tape
☐ Sublimation transfer (print/sheet)

EQUIPMENT
☐ Lint roller
☐ Flat heat source such as a heat press
☐ (Optional) Ruler or fabric tape measure for placement help

PREPARATION

Start with a new oven mitt for the best results. No need to pre-wash, but if you do, avoid fabric softener.

Pre-heat your flat heat press to the temperature shown in the chart below.

Very closely trim the edges of your sublimation transfer to minimize the appearance of paper lines on your finished oven mitt.

Use the lint roller to remove any extra pieces of fiber or fluff in the area you want to press.

Press the oven mitt with your heat press for 5 seconds to pre-heat it and remove any moisture.

Tape all four edges of your design face down on your oven mitt. A ruler may help with placement.

Place a sheet of blowout paper inside the oven mitt to prevent the ink from bleeding onto the other side.

Place a piece of blowout paper (I recommend white cardstock or butcher paper) on your pressing pad, then lay the oven mitt on top of the blowout paper. **Cover with another sheet of blowout paper.**

Press according to the chart below. Pull the transfer sheet while still warm.

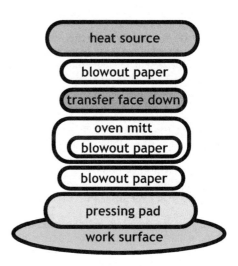

heat source
blowout paper
transfer face down
oven mitt
blowout paper
blowout paper
pressing pad
work surface

COOK TIMES
Here are typical times you can use as a starting point. Always check the manufacturer's instructions for time and temperature, when available.

your favorite settings

Traditional Heat Press	AutoPress	EasyPress	Mini Press	
385°F / 196°C	385°F / 196°C	385°F / 196°C	High	
45 seconds	45 seconds	45 seconds	55 seconds	
40 psi (medium pressure)	Auto pressure	Medium pressure	Heavy pressure	

TIPS & TRICKS
✓ Remember to mirror the design before printing your sublimation transfer.
✓ Make sure you are using enough pressure to flatten the oven mitt down as much as possible. If not flattened enough, it may result in ghosting.
✗ Don't remove your sublimation transfer sheet for at least 10 seconds so it can cool down without ghosting.

FLOOR MATS POLYESTER

ALSO: Car mats, door mats

Customize a sublimatable floor mat using overlapping sublimation transfers for a full-coverage design.

INGREDIENTS
☐ Polyester floor mat
☐ Blowout paper (several sheetsheets)
☐ Heat-resistant tape
☐ Sublimation transfer (print/sheet)

EQUIPMENT
☐ Lint roller
☐ Flat heat source such as a heat press
☐ Large stiff piece of cardboard
☐ (Optional) Ruler for placement help

PREPARATION

Start with a new floor mat for the best results. Use a lint roller to clean the mat.

Pre-heat your flat heat press to the temperature shown in chart below.

Pre-heat your mat for 5 seconds to remove any moisture.

If your design covers more than one transfer sheet, lay all of your sublimation transfer sheets face up on your work surface so the design is aligned. In this recipe, the design has four transfer sheets. For convenience, the top left sheet is numbered 1, top right sheet is 2, bottom left sheet is 3, and bottom right sheet is 4.

Next, trim the right and bottom edges of the Sheet 1. Trim the bottom edge of Sheet 2. Line Sheets 1 and 2 up, with the right edge of Sheet 1 overlapping the white left edge of Sheet 2. There should be no more white showing. **Secure in place with heat-resistant tape.**

Trim the right edge of Sheet 3. Line it up with Sheet 4, so the right edge of Sheet 3 overlaps the left edge of Sheet 4. There should be no more white showing. **Secure in place with heat-resistant tape.**

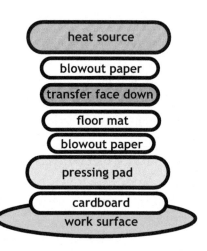

Line Sheets 1 and 2 up with Sheets 3 and 4. Overlap the top edges of Sheets 3 and 4 with the bottom edges of Sheets 1 and 2 so no more white is showing. **Secure in place with heat-resistant tape.**

Lay your floor mat face up and place the transfer face down on it. Secure in place with heat resistant tape.

Lay the piece of stiff cardboard on your heat press, then place the pressing mat on top. Cover the pressing pad with blowout paper (I recommend white cardstock or butcher paper). **Place the floor mat face up on the blowout paper.** Cover with more blowout paper.

Press according to the chart below. Pull the transfer sheet while still warm.

COOK TIMES

Here are typical times you can use as a starting point. Always check the manufacturer's instructions for time and temperature, when available.

your favorite settings

Traditional Heat Press	AutoPress	EasyPress	Mini Press	
390°F / 199°C	390°F / 199°C	390°F / 199°C	High	
70 seconds	70 seconds	70 seconds	90 seconds	
30 psi (light pressure)	Auto pressure	Light pressure	Light pressure	

TIPS & TRICKS
✓ For a tutorial on sublimating floor mats check out jennifermaker.com/how-to-sublimate-large-designs/

SEQUIN PILLOWS POLYESTER

ALSO: Sequin stockings, sequin shirts

This recipe is for a sublimation-ready sequin pillow cover or similiar items.

INGREDIENTS
☐ Sequin pillow covers
☐ Heat-resistant tape
☐ Blowout paper (two sheets)
☐ Sublimation transfer (print/sheet)

EQUIPMENT
☐ Lint Roller
☐ Flat heat source
☐ (Optional) Pillow or foam for items with zippers that might hinder a flat press

PREPARATION

Pre-heat your flat heat press to the temperature shown in the chart below.

Print and trim the edges of your printed sublimation transfer to minimize the appearance of paper lines on your finished pillow.

Lint roll the pillow's front to remove any dust and debris. **Push all sequins** so that only the white sides show and lint roll to remove anything loose.

Slide a piece of blowout paper (I recommend white cardstock or butcher paper) inside the pillow cover. Put the pillow cover on the pressing area, making sure that the **zipper head is outside of the pressing area.**

When the press is ready, pre-heat your pillow cover for 10 seconds.

Place your design in the middle of the cover, and measure the width to find the center of the cover. Then measure and find the middle from the top.

Place the design face down and use the heat-resistant tape to hold the sublimation print in place.

Cover the pillow with a clean sheet of **blowout paper and press.**

When the time is up, remove the butcher paper. When the pillow has cooled, **carefully peel away the tape and see your result.**

Place a pillow insert inside the pillow case and zip it up.

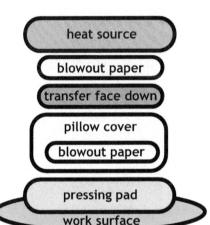

heat source
blowout paper
transfer face down
pillow cover
blowout paper
pressing pad
work surface

COOK TIMES
Here are typical times you can use as a starting point. Always check the manufacturer's instructions for time and temperature, when available.

your favorite settings

Traditional Heat Press	AutoPress	EasyPress	Mini Press	
360°F / 182°C	400°F / 204°C	385°F / 196°C	High	
120 seconds	60 seconds	45 seconds	75 seconds	
40 psi (medium pressure)	Auto pressure	Medium pressure	Medium pressure	

TIPS & TRICKS
✗ Don't remove your sublimation transfer sheet for at least 10 seconds so it can cool down without ghosting.
✓ If you plan to sublimate on both sides of the pillow, do the sequined side first.
✓ If you're pressing a sublimation design over seams, medium to firm pressure works better.
✓ After Care: To protect sequins, handwash the pillow cover.

CANVAS PILLOWS POLYESTER
ALSO: 100% polyester canvas tote bags

This recipe is a for a 100% polyester sublimation ready canvas pillow.

INGREDIENTS
☐ Canvas pillow cover (100% Polyester)
☐ Blowout paper (two sheets)
☐ Heat-resistant tape
☐ Sublimation transfer (print/sheet)

EQUIPMENT
☐ Lint roller
☐ Flat heat source such as a heat press
☐ (Optional) Ruler for placement help

PREPARATION

Start with a new canvas pillow cover. No need to pre-wash.

Pre-heat your flat heat press to the temperature shown in the chart below.

Trim the edges of your printed sublimation transfer to minimize the appearance of lines on your finished pillow cover.

Slide a piece of blowout paper (I recommend white cardstock or butcher paper) inside the pillow. Put the cover on the pressing area, making sure that the **zipper head is outside of the pressing area.**

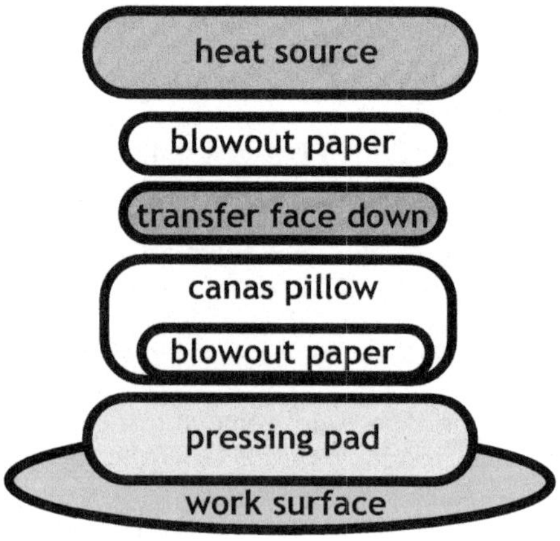

Lint roll the pillow cover to remove any dust and debris.

When the press is ready, pre-heat your pillowcase for 15 seconds.

Place your design in the middle, and measure the width to find the center of the cover. Then measure halfway from the top to find the center placement.

Place the design face down and use the heat resistant tape to hold the sublimation print in place.

Cover the pillow with a clean sheet of **blowout paper and press.**

When the time is up remove the butcher paper. When the pillow has cooled, **carefully peel away the tape and see your result.**

Place a pillow insert inside the pillow case and zip it up.

| heat source |
| blowout paper |
| transfer face down |
| canas pillow |
| blowout paper |
| pressing pad |
| work surface |

COOK TIMES
Here are typical times you can use as a starting point. Always check the manufacturer's instructions for time and temperature, when available.

your favorite settings

Traditional Heat Press	AutoPress	EasyPress	Mini Press	
400°F / 204°C	400°F / 204°C	385°F / 196°C	High	
45 seconds	60 seconds	60 seconds	75 seconds	
40 psi (medium pressure)	Auto pressure	Light pressure	Light pressure	

TIPS & TRICKS
✗ Don't remove your sublimation transfer sheet for at least 10 seconds so it can cool down without ghosting.
✓ If your sublimation design is mostly black, you may want to add an extra 10-20 seconds.
✓ If you're pressing a sublimation design over seams, medium to firm pressure works better.

GARDEN FLAGS POLYESTER

ALSO: Car Flags, Party Flags

This recipe is for a sublimation-ready 100% polyester garden flags.

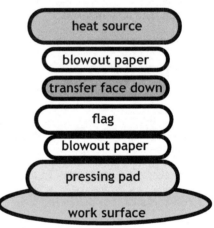

INGREDIENTS
☐ Sublimation garden flags (polyester)
☐ Heat-resistant tape
☐ Blowout paper (two sheets)
☐ Sublimation transfer (print/sheet)

EQUIPMENT
☐ Lint roller
☐ Flat heat source
☐ Pressing pad

PREPARATION

Pre-heat your flat heat press to the temperature shown in the chart below.

Print your sublimation transfer, making sure to add a bleed around the outside edges for full coverage. Then, **trim the edges of the transfer** to minimize the apperance of paper lines on your finished flag.

Lint roll the flag to remove any debris.

Slide a piece of blowout paper (I recommend white cardstock or butcher paper) under the flag.

When the press is ready, pre-heat your flag for 10 seconds.

Place your design in the middle, and measure the width to find the center of the garden flag. Then measure 10 inches from the top in the middle of the garden flag.

Place the design face down and use the heat-resistant tape to hold the sublimation print in place.

Cover the flag with a clean sheet of **blowout paper and press.**

When the time is up, remove the butcher paper. When the flag has cooled, **carefully peel away the tape and see your result.**

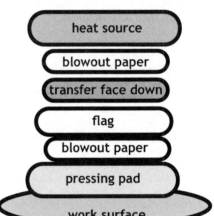

COOK TIMES
Here are typical times you can use as a starting point. Always check the manufacturer's instructions for time and temperature, when available.

your favorite settings

Traditional Heat Press	AutoPress	EasyPress	Mini Press	
400°F / 204°C	400°F / 204°C	380°F / 196°C	High	
60 seconds	55 seconds	60 seconds	75 seconds	
40 (Medium pressure)	Auto pressure	Medium pressure	Medium pressure	

TIPS & TRICKS
✗ Don't remove your sublimation transfer sheet for at least 10 seconds so it can cool down without ghosting.
✓ You can sublimate both sides of the flag simultaneously by creating a sublimation pocket, essentially having the sublimation print on both sides of the flag, pressing with the same temperature and increasing the time by 30 seconds.
✓ After Care: To safely wash your flag, it is recommended to use a gentle cycle with cold water and a mild detergent.

SOCKS POLYESTER

This recipe is for sublimation-ready socks. Depending on the material and the texture, some socks will sublimate better than others. Check your materials and print placement for the best results.

INGREDIENTS
- ☐ Sublimation socks
- ☐ Heat-resistant tape
- ☐ Blowout paper (two sheets)
- ☐ Sublimation transfer (print/sheet)

EQUIPMENT
- ☐ Lint roller
- ☐ Flat heat source such as a heat press
- ☐ Metal sock jig(s)
- ☐ (Optional) Ruler for placement

PREPARATION

Start with a new set of polyester socks. No need to pre-wash.

Pre-heat your flat heat press to the temperature shown in the chart below.

Tear or very closely trim the edges of your printed sublimation transfer to minimize the appearance of paper lines on your finished socks.

Prepare the sublimation surface by unfolding the socks and displaying the side that you want the design to be placed.

Wrap your sock jig with blowout paper to prevent transfer of ink to your jig, and then to another sock.

Slide a the sock jig inside each sock to stretch the sock to the right size.

Lint roll your socks to remove any dust or debris.

When the **press is ready,** pre-press your socks for 5 seconds to remove any moisture.

Using heat-resistant tape, secure all four edges of your design face down on your socks, a ruler can be used to help with placement.

Cover the socks with a piece of **blowout paper and press.**

Allow socks to cool before removing the transfer paper.

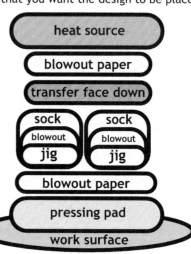

COOK TIMES
Here are typical times you can use as a starting point. Always check the manufacturer's instructions for time and temperature, when available.

your favorite settings

Traditional Heat Press	AutoPress	EasyPress	Mini Press	
400°F / 204°C	400°F / 204°C	385°F / 196°C	High	
60 seconds	45 seconds	40 seconds	75 seconds	
40 psi (medium pressure)	Auto pressure	Light pressure	Light pressure	

TIPS & TRICKS
- ✗ Don't remove your sublimation transfer sheet for at least 10 seconds so it can cool down without ghosting.
- ✓ If your socks are not white, you will need a darker sublimation design.
- ✓ If you're pressing a sublimation design over seams, medium to firm pressure works better.
- ✓ Projects and tutorial at jennifermaker.com/Dollar-Tree-Sublimation-Ideas/
- ✓ After Care: Machine wash: cold or warm, not hot. Gentle detergent. Dry: low heat or air-dry cycle.

STOCKINGS POLYESTER

This recipe is for a 100% polyester stocking. If you use a darker-colored stocking, you will want to use a darker-colored sublimation print.

INGREDIENTS
☐ Sublimation blank stocking
☐ Heat-resistant tape
☐ Blowout Paper (two sheets)
☐ Sublimation transfer (print/sheet)

EQUIPMENT
☐ Lint roller
☐ Flat heat source such as a heat press
☐ (Optional) Ruler for placement help

PREPARATION

Start with your new stocking. No need to pre-wash.

Pre-heat your flat heat press to the temperature shown in the chart below.

Trim the edges of your printed sublimation transfer to align with the edge of the stocking. If you are using an image that is not the size of the side of the stocking, you will want to trim the edges of the image to minimize the appearance of paper lines on your stocking.

Place blowout paper (I recommend white cardstock or butcher paper) inside the stocking, between the two layers of fabric.

Lint roll your stocking to remove any debris.

Place your **transfer paper** face down on your stocking.

Tape all four edges of your design face down on your stocking with heat-resistant tape. If you are not using a design that covers the whole side of the stocking, use a ruler to measure for appropriate placement.

Place blowout paper on top of the transfer sheet and press according to the time listed below.

Allow your **stocking to cool** before removing the transfer sheet to reveal your finished product.

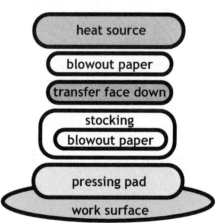

COOK TIMES

Here are typical times you can use as a starting point. Always check the manufacturer's instructions for time and temperature, when available.

your favorite settings

Traditional Heat Press	AutoPress	EasyPress	Mini Press	
400°F / 204°C	400°F / 204°C	385°F / 196°C	High	
60 seconds	50 seconds	45 seconds	70 seconds	
40 psi (light/medium)	Auto pressure	Light pressure	Light pressure	

TIPS & TRICKS
✗ Don't remove your sublimation transfer sheet for at least 10 seconds so it can cool down without ghosting.
✓ Prepare your blowout paper by cutting it out in the shape of the stocking.
✓ If you're pressing a sublimation design over seams, medium to firm pressure works better.
✓ After Care: It is recommended to wash the stockings by hand and line dry to maintain shape of the stocking.

FACE MASKS POLYESTER

ALSO: Sleepmasks

This recipe is for sublimation-ready face masks, but can also be used for sleep masks. Review item materials to ensure a high percentage of polyester on the sublimation side of the masks.

INGREDIENTS
☐ Sublimation blank face mask
☐ Blowout paper (two sheets)
☐ Heat-resistant tape
☐ Sublimation transfer (print/sheet)

EQUIPMENT
☐ Lint roller
☐ Flat heat source such as a heat press
☐ (Optional) Ruler for placement help

PREPARATION

Start with a sublimation ready face masks. For easier sublimation, your mask should have a flat surface area to sublimate on.

Pre-heat your flat heat press to the temperature shown in chart below.

Very closely trim the edges of your printed sublimation transfer to minimize the apperance of paper lines on your finished face mask.

Prepare the sublimation surface by placing a pressing pad, blowout paper (I recommend white cardstock or butcher paper), and then the face mask with the side that you want the sublimation print to show on your work surface.

Lint roll your mask to remove any dust or debris.

Then pre-press your face mask for 5 seconds.

Place your **sublimation transfer** on the face mask.

Using heat-resistant tape, secure all four edges of your design face down on your masks to help prevent ghosting during sublimation.

Cover the face masks and transfer print with blowout paper and press according to chart below.

Allow to cool before removing transfer sheet.

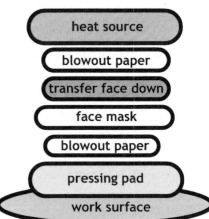

heat source
blowout paper
transfer face down
face mask
blowout paper
pressing pad
work surface

COOK TIMES
Here are typical times you can use as a starting point. Always check the manufacturer's instructions for time and temperature, when available.

your favorite settings

Traditional Heat Press	AutoPress	EasyPress	Mini Press	
375°F / 190°C	385°F / 196°C	385°F / 196°C	High	
45 seconds	45 seconds	40 seconds	70 seconds	
30 psi (light pressure)	Auto pressure	Light pressure	Light pressure	

TIPS & TRICKS
✗ Don't remove your sublimation transfer sheet for at least 10 seconds so it can cool down without ghosting.
✓ Masks that have folds can also be sublimated using a hat press will help with maintaining the masks shape.
✓ For masks that are 50% Cotton 50% Polyester, transfer onto the "shiny" polyester side.

STANDARD PATCH
POLYESTER

This recipe is for a standard patch with an adhesive backing. Because the patch already has adhesive backing, the sublimation transfer will be pressed onto the patch at the same time that the patch is pressed onto a backpack. The patch can be pressed on other items.

INGREDIENTS
☐ White polyester patch
☐ Backpack
☐ Blowout paper
☐ Heat-resistant tape
☐ Sublimation transfer (print/sheet)

EQUIPMENT
☐ Lint roller
☐ Flat heat source such as a heat press
☐ (Optional) Ruler for placement help

PREPARATION

Start with a new patch for best results. **Use a lint roller** to remove any dust or debris on the patch. **Use the lint roller** on the backpack as well.

Pre-heat your flat heat press to the temperature shown in chart below.

Very closely trim the edges of your printed sublimation transfer to match the size of your patch.

Pre-press the backpack for 10 seconds to remove any moisture. Leave it on the pressing pad.

Place your sublimation transfer design face down on top of the patch & secure it in place using heat-resistant tape.

Flip the patch over and remove the paper backing. **Place the patch face up** on the backpack. The adhesive backing should be against the backpack.

Place a sheet of blowout paper on top of the patch.

Press according to the chart below.

Remove blowout paper and sublimation transfer sheet while still warm.

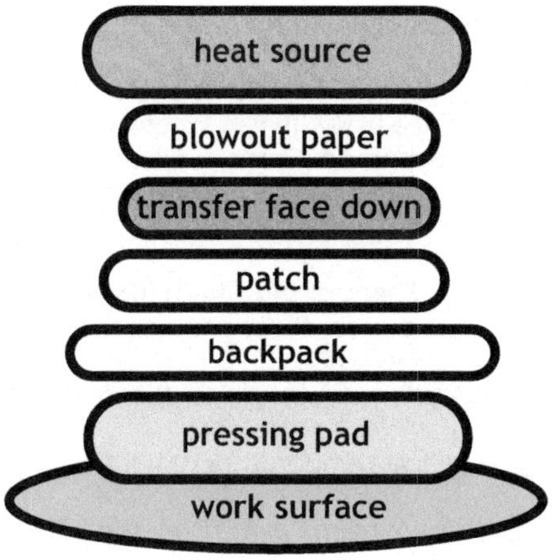

heat source
blowout paper
transfer face down
patch
backpack
pressing pad
work surface

COOK TIMES
Here are typical times you can use as a starting point. Always check the manufacturer's instructions for time and temperature, when available.

your favorite settings

Traditional Heat Press	AutoPress	EasyPress	Mini Press	
385°F / 196°C	385°F / 196°C	385°F / 196°C	High	
30 seconds	30 seconds	30 seconds	30 seconds	
40 psi (medium pressure)	Auto pressure	Medium pressure	Medium pressure	

TIPS & TRICKS
✗ Don't remove your sublimation transfer sheet for at least 10 seconds so it can cool down without ghosting.
✗ Don't press the patch separately if it has an adhesive backing.
✓ After Care: Wash with regular laundry and tumble dry.

FRINGED PATCH POLYESTER

This recipe is for a fringed patch of any shape with a separate adhesive strip. The sublimation transfer will be pressed onto the patch before pressing the patch onto a canvas tote, but can be pressed on other items.

INGREDIENTS
☐ Sublimation blank fringed patch
☐ Canvas tote
☐ Adhesive strip (comes with patch)
☐ Blowout paper
☐ Heat-resistant tape
☐ Sublimation transfer (print/sheet)

EQUIPMENT
☐ Lint roller
☐ Flat heat source such as a heat press
☐ (Optional) Ruler for placement help

PREPARATION

Start with a new sublimation-ready frayed patch for best restults. **Use a lint roller** to clean any dust or debris off the patch. Use the lint roller on the canvas tote as well.

Pre-heat your flat heat press to the temperature shown in chart below.

Very closely trim the edges of your printed sublimation transfer to match the size of your fringed patch.

Place your sublimation transfer design face down on the patch and secure it in place using heat-resistant tape. **Make sure none of the fringe pieces are stuck underneath the transfer.** If there are any pieces underneath the transfer, remove the transfer, move the fringe, and tape the transfer back down.

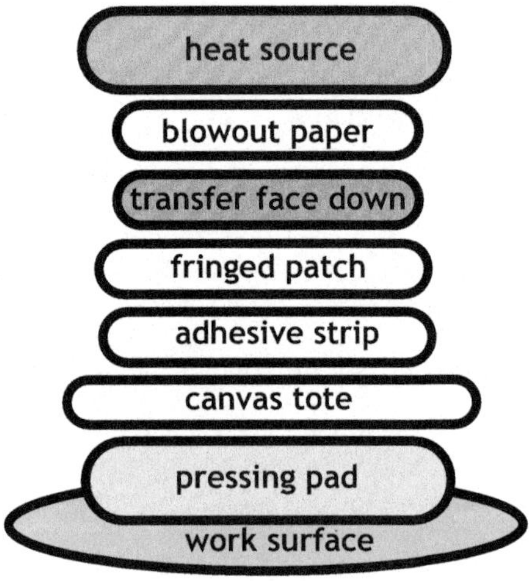

Place a sheet of blowout paper on your pressing pad, then **place the patch face up** on top. Place another sheet of blowout paper over the patch.

Press according to the chart below. **Let the patch cool completely.**

Lower the temperature of your heat press to 330°F / 166°C.

Peel the backing away from the adhesive strip. **Place the adhesive strip** on the canvas tote in the location you want the patch to be.

Lay the patch face up on top of the adhesive strip.

Cover the patch and canvas tote with a sheet of blowout paper.

Press for 30 seconds at medium pressure. Let cool slightly, then remove blowout paper.

heat source
blowout paper
transfer face down
fringed patch
adhesive strip
canvas tote
pressing pad
work surface

COOK TIMES
Here are typical times you can use as a starting point. Always check the manufacturer's instructions for time and temperature, when available.

your favorite settings

Traditional Heat Press	AutoPress	EasyPress	Mini Press	
385°F / 196°C	385°F / 196°C	385°F / 196°C	High	
60 seconds	60 seconds	60 seconds	60 seconds	
50 psi (heavy pressure	Auto pressure	Heavy pressure	Heavy pressure	

TIPS & TRICKS
✗ Don't remove your sublimation transfer sheet for at least 10 seconds so it can cool down without ghosting.
✓ After Care: Wash with regular laundry and tumble dry.

SEQUIN PATCH POLYESTER

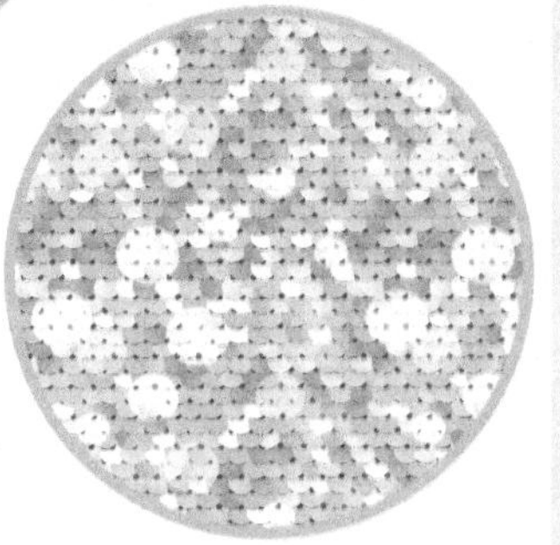

This recipe is for a sublimation-ready sequin patch with an adhesive backing. Because the patch has an adhesive backing, the sublimation transfer will be pressed onto the patch at the same time the patch is pressed onto a denim jacket. The patch can be pressed on other items.

INGREDIENTS
☐ Sublimation blank sequin patch
☐ Denim jacket
☐ Blowout paper
☐ Heat-resistant tape
☐ Sublimation transfer (print/sheet)

EQUIPMENT
☐ Lint roller
☐ Flat heat source such as a heat press
☐ (Optional) Ruler for placement help

PREPARATION

Start with a new sublimation-ready sequin patch for best results.

Pre-heat your flat heat press to the temperature shown in chart below.

Very closely trim the edges of your printed sublimation transfer to match the size of your sequin patch.

Flip all of the sequins on the patch so the white sides are showing.

Use a lint roller to remove any dust or debris on the patch. Be sure to **only lint roll in one direction** so the white sides of the sequins stay in place.

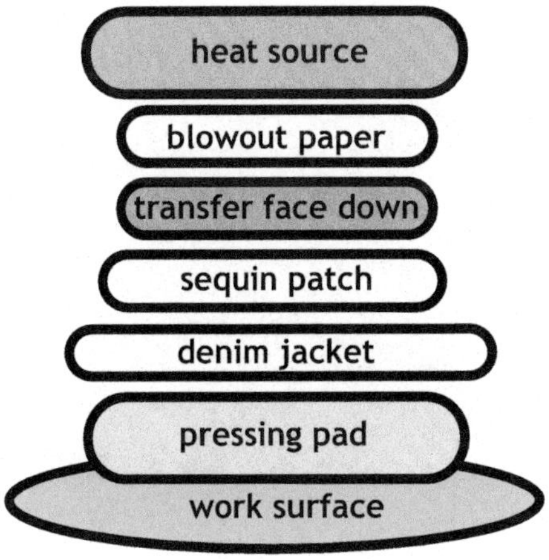

Use the lint roller on the denim jacket as well.

Pre-press the denim jacket for 10 seconds to remove any moisture. Leave it on the pressing pad.

Place your sublimation transfer design face down on top of the sequined patch & secure it in place using heat-resistant tape.

Flip the sequined patch over and remove the paper backing. **Place the patch face up** on the denim jacket. The adhesive backing should be against the denim jacket.

Place a sheet of blowout paper on top of the patch.

Press according to the chart below.

Remove blowout paper and sublimation transfer sheet while still warm.

| heat source |
| blowout paper |
| transfer face down |
| sequin patch |
| denim jacket |
| pressing pad |
| work surface |

COOK TIMES
Here are typical times you can use as a starting point. Always check the manufacturer's instructions for time and temperature, when available.

your favorite settings

Traditional Heat Press	AutoPress	EasyPress	Mini Press	
360°F / 182°C	360°F / 182°C	360°F / 182°C	High	
90 seconds	90 seconds	90 seconds	90 seconds	
40 psi (medium pressure)	Auto pressure	Medium pressure	Medium pressure	

TIPS & TRICKS
✗ Don't remove your sublimation transfer sheet for at least 10 seconds so it can cool down without ghosting.
✓ After Care: Wash with regular laundry and tumble dry.

CHAPTER 2
STAINLESS STEEL

STRAIGHT-SIDED TUMBLERS
STAINLESS STEEL

This recipe calls for a straight-sided tumbler, such as a skinny tumbler, that is sublimation-ready.

INGREDIENTS
☐ Straight-sided tumbler (stainless-steel)
☐ Butcher paper (one sheet)
☐ Heat-resistant tape
☐ Sublimation transfer (print/sheet)

EQUIPMENT
☐ Lint-free cloth
☐ Rubbing alcohol
☐ Heat source appropriate for tumblers
☐ (Optional) Shrink wrap and heat gun
☐ (Optional) Silicone bands

PREPARATION

Use a lint-free cloth and rubbing alcohol to clean the tumbler.

Trim the top, bottom, and right edges of the sublimation transfer at the edge of the ink so no white edges are visible. **Trim the left edge** to leave a quarter-inch strip of white.

Wrap the sublimation transfer around the tumbler so the ink touches the surface. The transfer should overlap slightly. Firmly tape the transfer to itself, then tape along the seam, leaving an inch or so untaped along the top and bottom.

Press hard and smooth the paper from both sides toward the seam. If anything ripples, remove the tape and try again. **Add tape to cover your seam's top and bottom remainders, allowing some of the tape to fold over the top and bottom edges.** Use a scraper to thoroughly work air pockets out.

Firmly tape the transfer along all the top and bottom edges of the tumbler. **Tape the top, bottom, left, and right edges** as though following directions on a compass. **Rotate the tumbler slightly** and repeat until the design transfer is completely covered. The edges of the tape should fold over into the tumbler at the top and onto the bottom of the tumbler.

Wrap the tumbler in a piece of butcher paper, securing with tape. If using shrink wrap (not to be used in a tumbler press), do this after the butcher paper layer.

Press according to the chart below. Pull the transfer sheet while still warm.

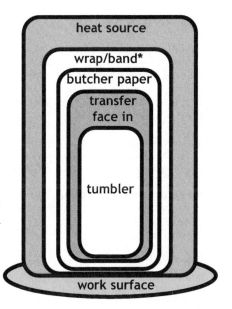

COOK TIMES
Here are typical times you can use as a starting point. Always check the manufacturer's instructions for time and temperature, when available.

your favorite settings

Tumbler Press	Convection Oven	Air Fryer	
360°F / 176°C	375°F / 190°C	385°F / 196°C	
100 seconds	6 minutes	6 minutes	
40 psi (medium pressure)			

TIPS & TRICKS
✓ Always use heat-resistant gloves when placing/removing your tumbler in/from the heat source.
✓ Before heating your tumbler press, adjust the tension to ensure a snug fit with your tumbler.
✗ Don't pull shrink wrap overly tight. This risks it pulling apart in the oven.
✓ For a tutorial check out jennifermaker.com/sublimation-tumblers/

TAPERED TUMBLERS
STAINLESS STEEL
ALSO: Cupholder tumblers

Create a beautiful tapered tumbler by slightly altering the recipe for the straight-sided tumbler.

INGREDIENTS
☐ Tapered tumbler (stainless steel)
☐ Butcher paper (one sheet)
☐ Heat-resistant tape
☐ Sublimation transfer (print/sheet)

EQUIPMENT
☐ Lint-free cloth
☐ Rubbing alcohol
☐ Heat source appropriate for tumblers
☐ (Optional) Shrink wrap and heat gun
☐ (Optional) Silicone bands

PREPARATION

Use a lint-free cloth and rubbing alcohol to clean the tumbler.

Use a tapered template for the sublimation transfer design, which has a wider top, a narrower bottom, and curved edges.

Trim the top, bottom, and right edges of the sublimation transfer at the edge of the ink so no white edges are visible. Trim the left edge to leave a quarter-inch strip of white.

Wrap the sublimation transfer around the tumbler so the ink touches the surface. The transfer should overlap slightly. Firmly tape the transfer to itself, then tape along the seam, leaving an inch or so untaped along the top and bottom.

Press hard and smooth the paper from both sides toward the seam. If anything ripples, remove the tape and try again. Add tape to cover the top and bottom remainders of your seam, allowing some of the tape to fold over the top and bottom edges. Use a scraper to thoroughly work air pockets out.

Firmly tape the transfer along all the top and bottom edges of the tumbler. Tape the top, bottom, left, and right edges as though following directions on a compass. Rotate the tumbler slightly and repeat until the design transfer is completely covered. The edges of the tape should fold over into the tumbler at the top and onto the bottom of the tumbler.

Wrap the tumbler in a piece of butcher paper, securing with tape. If using shrink wrap (not to be used in a tumbler press), do this after the butcher paper layer.

Press according to the chart below. Pull the transfer sheet while still warm.

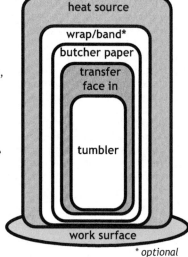

heat source
wrap/band*
butcher paper
transfer
face in

tumbler

work surface

optional

COOK TIMES
Here are typical times you can use as a starting point. Always check the manufacturer's instructions for time and temperature, when available.

your favorite settings

Tumbler Press	Convection Oven	Air Fryer	
360°F / 182°C	375°F / 190°C	385°F / 196°C	
100 seconds	6 minutes	6 minutes	
40 psi (medium pressure)			

TIPS & TRICKS
✗ Don't pull shrink wrap overly tight. This risks it pulling apart in the oven.
✓ If using a tumbler press or air fryer, turn the tumbler 180 degrees halfway through the cooking time.
✗ If your transfer edges do not line up around the tumbler, you likely did not use a tapered template.

CAMPING MUGS STAINLESS STEEL

This recipe allows you to make a vessel to use in front of a crackling open fire, using a sublimation-ready camping mug.

INGREDIENTS
☐ Camping mug (stainless steel)
☐ Butcher paper (one sheet)
☐ Heat-resistant tape
☐ Sublimation transfer (print/sheet)

EQUIPMENT
☐ Lint-free cloth
☐ Rubbing alcohol
☐ Heat source appropriate for tumblers & mugs
☐ (Optional) Shrink wrap and heat gun
☐ (Optional) Silicone bands or silicone wrap

PREPARATION

Use a lint-free cloth and rubbing alcohol to clean the camping mug.

Pre-heat your heat press to the temperature shown in the chart below.

Trim the edges of the sublimation transfer to eliminate excess paper and ensure a good fit on the camping mug.

Wrap the sublimation transfer around the mug so the ink touches the surface. How much of the mug is covered depends on whether your design is only on one side or from handle-to-handle. For a full-mug design, **place the mug with the handle facing you** and place the center of the design on the opposite side, smoothing each side as it moves toward the handle.

Firmly tape the transfer to itself underneath the handle. Then, secure the rest of the transfer to the mug by applying heat-resistant tape to the edges. **Tape the top, bottom, left, and right edges** as though following directions on a compass. **Rotate the mug slightly** and repeat until the design transfer is completely covered. The edges of the tape should fold over into the mug at the top and onto the bottom of the mug. Use a scraper to thoroughly work air pockets out.

Wrap the mug in a piece of butcher paper, securing with tape. If using a shrink wrap (not to be used in a tumbler press), do this after the butcher paper layer.

Press according to the chart below. Pull the transfer sheet while still warm.

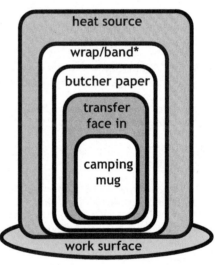

heat source

wrap/band*

butcher paper

transfer face in

camping mug

work surface

COOK TIMES
Here are typical times you can use as a starting point. Always check the manufacturer's instructions for time and temperature, when available.

your favorite settings

Tumbler Press	Convection Oven	Air Fryer	
385°F /196°C	375°F / 190°C	385°F / 196°C	
120 seconds	6 minutes	6 minutes	
40 psi (medium pressure)			

TIPS & TRICKS
✓ Always use heat-resistant gloves when placing/removing your tumbler in/from the heat source.
✓ If your camping mug has a lip and you are using a tumbler press, place the lip just outside of the edge of the tumbler press, with the rest of the mug inside the press.
✓ If using the Cricut Mug Press in conjuction with a camping mug with a lip, it may be helpful to wrap the camping mug with silicone bands or a silicone wrap to achieve a more snug fit.

FLASKS STAINLESS STEEL

Personalize a sublimation-ready stainless steel flask as a gift for events, such as groomsman gifts or birthdays.

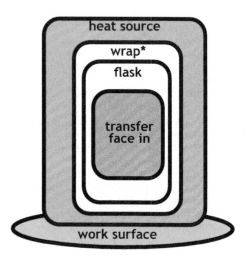

INGREDIENTS
☐ Flask (stainless steel)
☐ Butcher paper (one sheet)
☐ Heat-resistant tape
☐ Sublimation transfer (print/sheet)

EQUIPMENT
☐ Lint-free cloth
☐ Rubbing alcohol
☐ Heat source
☐ (Optional) Shrink wrap and heat gun
☐ (Optional) Silicone flask wrap

PREPARATION

Pre-heat your heat press to the temperature shown in the chart below.

Remove the cap of the flask and set it aside. Do not put it into the heat source.

Trim the edges of the sublimation transfer to eliminate excess paper and ensure a good fit on the flask.

Place the sublimation transfer face down on the front of the flask. Make sure it is smooth against the surface of the flask before applying tape.

Firmly tape the transfer to the flask by applying heat-resistant tape to each of the edges. Use a scraper to thoroughly work air pockets out.

Wrap a piece of butcher paper around the flask. Secure it with heat-resistant tape.

For best results, wrap the flask in either shrink wrap using a heat gun, or use a silicone flask wrap.

Press according to the chart below. Pull the transfer sheet while still warm.

COOK TIMES
Here are typical times you can use as a starting point. Always check the manufacturer's instructions for time and temperature, when available.

your favorite settings

Convection Oven	Air Fryer	
375°F / 190°C	385°F / 196°C	
6 minutes	6 minutes	

TIPS & TRICKS
✗ Don't remove your sublimation transfer sheet for at least 10 seconds so it can cool down without ghosting.
✓ Although you can put your flask into the heat source without a silicone wrap or shrink wrap, results are not guaranteed.
✓ Once you are finished sublimating the flask, remember to put the cap back on.

INSULATED CAN COOLERS
STAINLESS STEEL

This recipe uses a sublimation-ready stainless steel can cooler. Be a star host at your next BBQ by providing custom-designed can coolers!

INGREDIENTS
☐ Insulated can cooler (stainless steel)
☐ Butcher paper (one sheet)
☐ Heat-resistant tape
☐ Sublimation transfer (print/sheet)

EQUIPMENT
☐ Lint-free cloth
☐ Rubbing alcohol
☐ Heat source appropriate for tumblers
☐ (Optional) Shrink wrap and heat gun
☐ (Optional) Silicone bands

PREPARATION

Use a lint-free cloth and rubbing alcohol to clean the tumbler.

If your can cooler has a top that unscrews from the body, remove it and set it aside before wrapping your insulated can cooler.

Trim the top, bottom, and right edges of the sublimation transfer at the edge of the ink so no white edges are visible. **Trim the left edge** to leave a quarter-inch strip of white.

Wrap the sublimation transfer around the can cooler so the ink touches the surface. The transfer should overlap slightly. Firmly tape the transfer to itself, then tape along the seam, leaving an inch or so untaped along the top and bottom.

Press hard and smooth the paper from both sides toward the seam. If anything ripples, remove tape and try again. **Add tape to cover the top and bottom remainders of your seam,** allowing some of the tape to fold over the top and bottom edges. Use a scraper to thoroughly work air pockets out.

Firmly tape the transfer along all the top and bottom edges of the can cooler Tape the top, bottom, left, and right edges as though following directions on a compass. Rotate the can cooler slightly and repeat until the design transfer is completely covered. The edges of the tape should fold over into the can cooler at the top, as well as onto the bottom of the can cooler. Use a scraper to thoroughly work air pockets out.

Wrap the tumbler in a piece of butcher paper, securing with tape. If using a shrink wrap (not to be used in a tumbler press), do this after the butcher paper layer.

Press according to the chart below. Pull the transfer sheet while still warm.

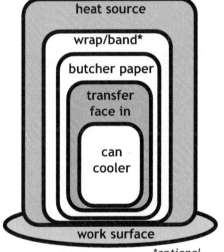

heat source
wrap/band*
butcher paper
transfer face in
can cooler
work surface

optional

COOK TIMES
Here are typical times you can use as a starting point. Always check the manufacturer's instructions for time and temperature, when available.

your favorite settings

Tumbler Press	Convection Oven	Air Fryer	
365°F / 185°C	375°F / 190°C	385°F / 196°C	
45 seconds	6 minutes	6 minutes	
40 psi (medium pressure)			

TIPS & TRICKS
✗ Don't forget to remove the unscrewable top before wrapping and sublimating. The tops are often plastic and will melt in the heat source. Once your insulated can cooler is no longer hot, place the top back on.

CHAPTER 3
CERAMIC

MUGS (WITH HANDLES) CERAMIC

Customize a sublimation-ready mug with your favorite photo, image, or phrase by following this recipe. Most mugs come in 11 oz. and 15 oz. sizes.

INGREDIENTS
☐ Ceramic mug
☐ Butcher paper (one sheet)
☐ Heat-resistant tape
☐ Sublimation transfer (print/sheet)

EQUIPMENT
☐ Lint roller
☐ Heat source appropriate for mugs
☐ (Optional) Silicone wrap

PREPARATION

Use a lint roller to clean the surface of the mug.

Pre-heat your heat press to the temperature shown in the chart below.

Trim the edges of the sublimation transfer to eliminate excess paper and ensure a good fit on the mug.

Wrap the sublimation transfer around the mug so that the ink touches the surface. **Place the mug with the handle facing you** and place the center of the transfer on the opposite side, smoothing each side as it moves toward the handle.

Using heat-resistant tape, secure the right edge of the transfer from top to bottom. Make sure that the transfer lays smoothly against the mug, then tape the left edge from top to bottom. Use a scraper to thoroughly work out any air pockets.

Wrap the mug in a piece of butcher paper, securing with tape. If using a silicone wrap, do this after the butcher paper layer.

Press according to the chart below. Pull the transfer sheet while still warm.

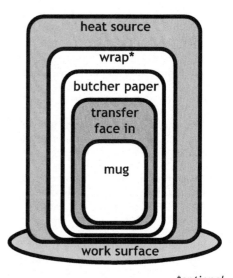

heat source
wrap*
butcher paper
transfer face in
mug
work surface

optional

COOK TIMES
Here are typical times you can use as a starting point. Always check the manufacturer's instructions for time and temperature, when available.

your favorite settings

Cricut Mug Press	Tumbler Press	Convection Oven	Air Fryer	
Auto temperature	400°F / 204°C	400°F / 204°C	400°F / 204°C	
Auto time	270 seconds	15 minutes	8-9 minutes	
Auto pressure	40 psi (medium pressure)			

TIPS & TRICKS
✗ Butcher paper is not needed if using infusible ink sheets.
✓ If using a convection oven or air fryer, turn your mug 180 degrees halfway through the cooking time.
✓ For a tutorial check out jennifermaker.com/cricut-mug-press-sublimation-blanks/

MUGS (NO HANDLES)
CERAMIC
ALSO: Pencil cups

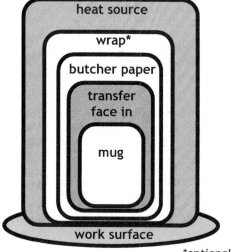

A sublimation-ready ceramic mug without a handle most often comes in 11 oz. and 15. oz. sizes, and is a perfect personalized drinking vessel or pencil cup.

INGREDIENTS
☐ Ceramic mug without a handle
☐ Butcher paper (one sheet)
☐ Heat-resistant tape
☐ Sublimation transfer (print/sheet)

EQUIPMENT
☐ Lint roller
☐ Heat source appropriate for mugs
☐ (Optional) Silicone wrap

PREPARATION

Use a lint roller to clean the surface of the mug.

Pre-heat your heat press to the temperature shown in the chart below.

Trim the top, bottom, and right edges of the sublimation transfer at the edge of the ink so no white edges are visible. **Trim the left edge** to leave a quarter-inch strip of white.

Wrap the sublimation transfer around the mug so the ink touches the surface. The transfer should overlap slightly. Firmly tape the transfer to itself, then tape along the seam, leaving an inch or so untaped along the top and bottom.

Press hard and smooth the paper from both sides toward the seam. If anything ripples, remove the tape and try again. **Add tape to cover the top and bottom remainders of your seam,** allowing some of the tape to fold over the top and bottom edges. Use a scraper to thoroughly work air pockets out.

Wrap the mug in a piece of butcher paper, securing with tape. If using a silicone wrap, do this after the butcher paper layer.

Press according to the chart below. Pull the transfer sheet while still warm.

Diagram labels, outer to inner:
heat source
wrap*
butcher paper
transfer face in
mug
work surface

*optional

COOK TIMES
Here are typical times you can use as a starting point. Always check the manufacturer's instructions for time and temperature, when available.

your favorite settings

Cricut Mug Press	Tumbler Press	Convection Oven	Air Fryer	
Auto temperature	400°F / 204°C	400°F / 204°C	400°F / 204°C	
Auto time	270 seconds	15 minutes	8-9 minutes	
Auto pressure	40 psi (medium pressure)			

TIPS & TRICKS
✓ If using a convection oven or air fryer, turn your mug 180 degrees halfway through the cooking time.
✓ For a tutorial check out jennifermaker.com/cricut-mug-press-sublimation-blanks/
✗ Don't remove your sublimation transfer sheet until the mug has cooled down.

CAMPING MUGS CERAMIC

Your sublimation-ready camping mug may have a lip made of ceramic, enamel, or stainless steel, all of which can withstand the temperature of your heat source.

INGREDIENTS
☐ Ceramic camping mug
☐ Butcher paper (one sheet)
☐ Heat-resistant tape
☐ Sublimation transfer (print/sheet)

EQUIPMENT
☐ Lint roller
☐ Heat source appropriate for mugs
☐ Heat-resistant gloves
☐ (Optional) Silicone wrap

PREPARATION

Use a lint roller to clean the camping mug.

Pre-heat your heat press to the temperature shown in the chart below.

Trim the edges of the sublimation transfer to eliminate excess paper and ensure a good fit on the camping mug.

Wrap the sublimation transfer around the mug so the ink touches the surface. **Place the mug with the handle facing you** and place the center of the transfer on the opposite side, smoothing each side as it moves toward the handle.

Using heat-resistant tape, secure the right edge of the transfer from top to bottom. Make sure that the transfer lays smoothly against the mug, then tape the left edge from top to bottom. Use a scraper to thoroughly work out any air pockets.

Wrap the mug in a piece of butcher paper, securing with tape. If using a silicone wrap, do this after the butcher paper layer.

Press according to the chart below. Pull the transfer sheet while still warm.

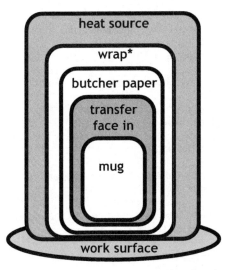

heat source
wrap*
butcher paper
transfer face in
mug
work surface

optional

COOK TIMES
Here are typical times you can use as a starting point. Always check the manufacturer's instructions for time and temperature, when available.

your favorite settings

Cricut Mug Press	Tumbler Press	Convection Oven	Air Fryer	
Auto temperature	400°F / 204°C	400°F / 204°C	400°F / 204°C	
Auto time	270 seconds	15 minutes	8-9 minutes	
Auto pressure	40 psi (medium pressure)			

TIPS & TRICKS
✗ Avoid placing your sublimation transfer on any curve below the lip of the camping mug, as this may cause undesirable results.
✓ If your camping mug has a lip and you are using a tumbler press, place the lip just outside of the edge of the tumbler press, with the rest of the mug inside the press.
✓ If using the Cricut Mug Press in conjunction with a camping mug with a lip, it may be helpful to wrap the camping mug with silicone bands or a silicone wrap to achieve a more snug fit.
✓ Always use heat-resistant gloves when placing/removing your camping mug in/from the heat source.

TILES CERAMIC

A sublimation-ready tile may be glossy or matte. Note that you cannot use tiles from the home improvement store or an old home project unless you coat them yourself with a sublimation-friendly layer, as ceramic is not naturally receptive to sublimation ink.

INGREDIENTS
☐ Flat ceramic tile
☐ Blowout paper (two sheets)
☐ Heat-resistant tape
☐ Sublimation transfer (print/sheet)

EQUIPMENT
☐ Lint roller
☐ Flat heat source such as a heat press

PREPARATION

Pre-heat your flat heat press to the temperature shown in the chart below.

Closely trim the edges of your sublimation transfer.

Use a lint roller to clean the surface of the tile.

Lay your sublimation transfer face up on your work surface. **Lay the tile face down** on top of it. The ink side of the sublimation transfer should be touching the face of the tile. Make sure the design is properly aligned with the tile and **secure the transfer in place using heat-resistant tape.**

Place a sheet of blowout paper (I recommend white cardstock or butcher paper) on the pressing pad.

Place the tile face down on the blowout paper. Lay another sheet of blowout paper on top of the tile.

Press according to the chart below. Pull the transfer sheet while still warm.

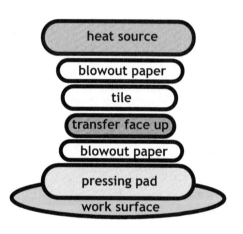

heat source
blowout paper
tile
transfer face up
blowout paper
pressing pad
work surface

COOK TIMES
Here are typical times you can use as a starting point. Always check the manufacturer's instructions for time and temperature, when available.

your favorite settings

Traditional Heat Press	AutoPress	EasyPress	Mini Press	
400°F / 204°C	400°F / 204°C	400°F / 204°C	High	
240 seconds	200 seconds	240 seconds	260 seconds	
30 psi (light pressure)	Auto pressure	Light pressure	Light pressure	

TIPS & TRICKS
✗ Don't remove your sublimation transfer sheet for at least 10 seconds so it can cool down without ghosting.
✓ Always check the manufacturer's recommended time and temperature for your tiles as the times especially can vary by several minutes.
✓ For flat ceramics, the blank is often pressed face down rather than face up.

ORNAMENTS CERAMIC

ALSO: Ceramic coasters, car coasters

Sublimation-ready ceramic ornaments come in a variety of shapes and can be used as more than just holiday decorations.

INGREDIENTS
☐ Flat ceramic ornament
☐ Blowout paper (two sheets)
☐ Heat-resistant tape
☐ Sublimation transfer (print/sheet)

EQUIPMENT
☐ Lint roller
☐ Flat heat source such as a heat press

PREPARATION

Pre-heat your flat heat press to the temperature shown in the chart below.

Check if your ornament has a liner on either side. This may be plastic or paper. If so, remove it. If your ornament comes with a ribbon, string, or other hanger attached, remove it as well.

Use the lint roller on the ceramic ornament to remove any debris.

Closely trim the edges of your sublimation transfer.

Position the sublimation transfer face up and place the ornament directly on top. The ink side of the transfer should be touching the face of the ceramic ornament. Make sure the design is properly aligned with the ornament and **secure the transfer in place using heat-resistant tape.**

Lay a sheet of blowout paper (I recommend white cardstock or butcher paper) on the pressing pad.

Place the ornament face down on the blowout paper. The sublimation transfer should be on the blowout paper, with the ceramic ornament on top of the transfer. **Place another sheet of blowout paper over the ornament.**

Press according to the chart below. Pull the transfer sheet while still warm.

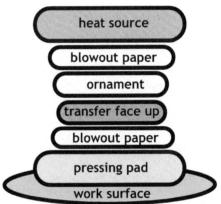

COOK TIMES
Here are typical times you can use as a starting point. Always check the manufacturer's instructions for time and temperature, when available.

your favorite settings

Traditional Heat Press	AutoPress	EasyPress	Mini Press		
400°F / 204°C	400°F / 204°C	400°F / 204°C	High		
160 seconds	200 seconds	240 seconds	260 seconds		
30 psi (light pressure)	Auto pressure	Light pressure	Light pressure		

TIPS & TRICKS
✗ Don't remove your sublimation transfer sheet for at least 10 seconds so it can cool down without ghosting.
✓ If using a ceramic ornament that is decoratively shaped, be sure to measure the widest points before creating a sublimation transfer design so that the ornament is fully covered.
✓ For flat ceramics, the blank is often pressed face down rather than face up.
✓ For a tutorial on sublimating ornaments check out jennifermaker.com/diy-sublimation-ornaments/

PLATES CERAMIC

ALSO: Ceramic charger plates, decorative display plates

Most sublimatable plates have curves, so they must be sublimated in either a convection oven or air fryer, or with the round puck attachment on a traditional heat press.

INGREDIENTS
☐ Ceramic plate
☐ Blowout paper (two sheets)
☐ Heat-resistant tape
☐ Sublimation transfer (print/sheet)

EQUIPMENT
☐ Lint roller
☐ Heat source appropriate for sublimating plates

PREPARATION

Pre-heat your heat source to the temperature shown in the chart below.

Closely trim the edges of your sublimation transfer.

Use a lint roller to clean the surface of the plate.

Place your sublimation transfer face down on the plate. Secure it in place with heat-resistant tape.

Place a sheet of blowout paper (I recommend white cardstock or butcher paper) on the pressing pad or base of the heat source.

Place the plate face up on top of the blowout paper.

If using a traditional heat press, place another sheet of blowout paper on top of the plate. If using a convection oven or air fryer, this step is not necessary.

Press according to the chart below. Pull the transfer sheet while still warm.

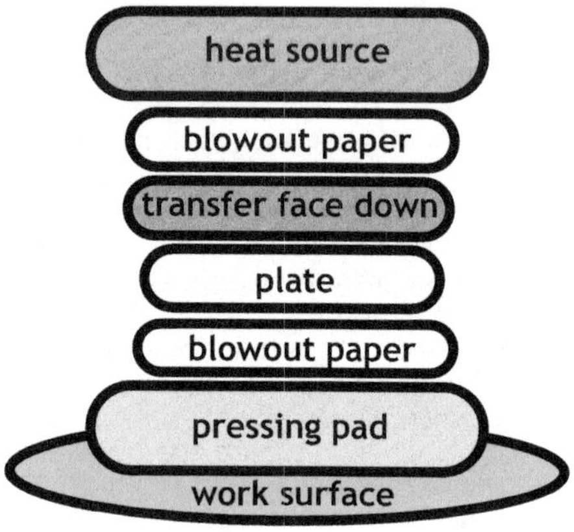

heat source
blowout paper
transfer face down
plate
blowout paper
pressing pad
work surface

COOK TIMES
Here are typical times you can use as a starting point. Always check the manufacturer's instructions for time and temperature, when available.

your favorite settings

Traditional Heat Press	Convection Oven	Air Fryer	
400°F / 204°C	400°F / 204°C	400°F / 204°C	
240 seconds	8 minutes	8 minutes	
30 psi (light pressure)			

TIPS & TRICKS
✗ Don't remove your sublimation transfer sheet for at least 10 seconds so it can cool down without ghosting.
✓ If using a traditional heat press, the round puck press is required.
✓ If your traditional heat press has more than one round puck option, choose the one that fits comfortably in the center of your plate.
✓ The round puck on a traditional heat press will only allow you to sublimate the flat center part of a plate.
✓ If using a convection oven or air fryer, rotate your plate 180 degrees halfway through the cooking time.

BOWLS CERAMIC

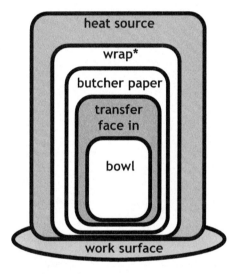

Sublimatable bowls must be sublimated in either a convection oven or an air fryer. Create a ceramic bowl for yourself or your furry best friend.

INGREDIENTS
☐ Ceramic bowl
☐ Blowout paper (two sheets)
☐ Heat-resistant tape
☐ Sublimation transfer (print/sheet)

EQUIPMENT
☐ Lint roller
☐ Heat source appropriate for sublimating bowls
☐ (Optional) Shrink wrap and heat gun
☐ (Optional) Silicone wrap

PREPARATION

Pre-heat your heat source to the temperature shown in the chart below.

Trim the top, bottom, and right edges of the sublimation transfer at the edge of the ink so no white edges are visible. **Trim the left edge** to leave a quarter-inch strip of white.

Use a lint roller to clean the outside surface of the bowl.

Wrap your sublimation transfer around the outside of the bowl so the ink touches the surface. The transfer should overlap slightly, with the quarter inch white strip on top. Firmly tape the transfer to itself, then tape along the seam, leaving an inch or so untaped along the top and bottom.

Firmly tape the transfer along all the top and bottom edges of the bowl. **Tape the top, bottom, left, and right edges** as though following directions on a compass. **Rotate the bowl slightly** and repeat until the design transfer is completely covered. The edges of the tape should fold over into the bowl at the top, as well as onto the bottom of the bowl.

Wrap the bowl in a piece of butcher paper, securing with tape. If using a silicone wrap, do this after the butcher paper layer.

Press according to the chart below. Pull the transfer sheet while still warm.

COOK TIMES
Here are typical times you can use as a starting point. Always check the manufacturer's instructions for time and temperature, when available.

your favorite settings

Convection Oven	Air Fryer	
400°F / 204°C	400°F / 204°C	
15 minutes	15 minutes	

TIPS & TRICKS
✓ Pay attention to the shape of the bowl to determine the shape of your sublimation transfer. A bowl with curved edges will require a tapered transfer, while a bowl with straight edges will not.
✗ Don't remove your sublimation transfer sheet for at least 10 seconds so it can cool down without ghosting.
✓ If using a convection oven or air fryer, rotate your bowl 180 degrees halfway through the cooking time.

CHAPTER 4
MDF & HDF

COASTERS MDF/HDF

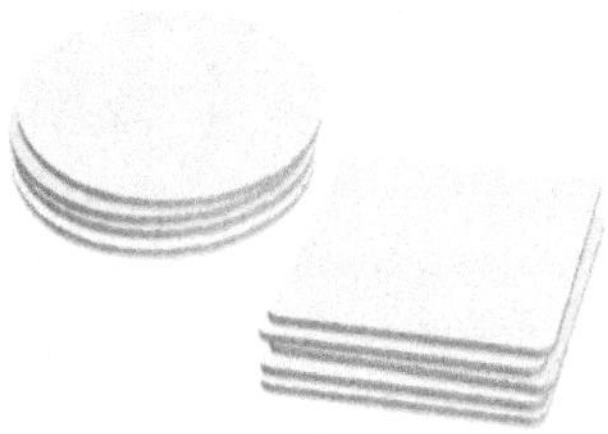

Sublimation-ready MDF and HDF coasters most often have a backing made of cork. These coasters most often come in round and square shapes.

INGREDIENTS
☐ MDF/HDF coaster of any shape
☐ Blowout paper (two sheets)
☐ Heat-resistant tape
☐ Sublimation transfer (print/sheet)

EQUIPMENT
☐ Lint roller
☐ Flat heat source such as a heat press

PREPARATION

Pre-heat your flat heat press to the temperature shown in the chart below.

Closely trim the edges of your sublimation transfer.

Check to see if there is a protective film or cover on your blank. It may be difficult to see, so check thoroughly. If so, remove it.

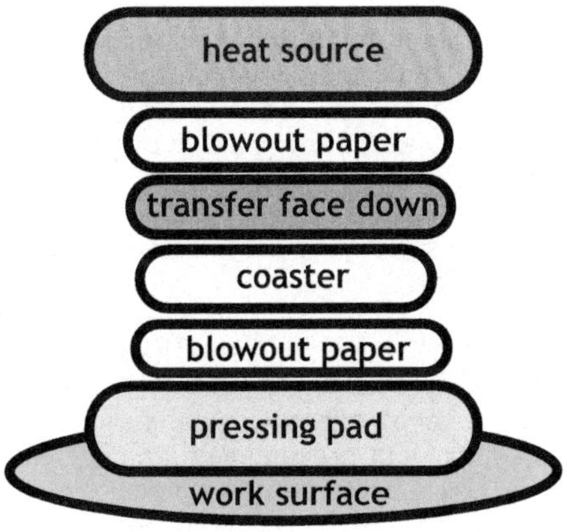

Use the lint roller on the surface of the coaster to clean it.

Place a sheet of blowout paper (I recommend white cardstock or butcher paper) on your pressing pad, and lay the coaster face up on top of it. Cover it with another piece of blowout paper and **pre-press it for 5 seconds to remove any moisture.**

Place the sublimation transfer face up on your work surface. **Lay the coaster face down** on top of the sublimation transfer and align it. Secure it in place with heat-resistant tape.

Place a sheet of blowout paper on the pressing pad.

Next, **place the coaster with the taped sublimation transfer facing up.**

Place another sheet of blowout paper on top.

Press according to the chart below. Pull the transfer sheet while still warm.

heat source
blowout paper
transfer face down
coaster
blowout paper
pressing pad
work surface

COOK TIMES
Here are typical times you can use as a starting point. Always check the manufacturer's instructions for time and temperature, when available.

your favorite settings

Traditional Heat Press	AutoPress	EasyPress	Mini Press	
400°F / 204°C	400°F / 204°C	390°F / 198°C	High	
60 seconds	50 seconds	50 seconds	60 seconds	
40 psi (medium pressure)	Auto pressure	Medium pressure	Medium pressure	

TIPS & TRICKS
× Don't remove your sublimation transfer sheet for at least 10 seconds so it can cool down without ghosting.
× If your coaster looks yellowish after pressing, try lowering the heat or cook time slightly.

PICTURE FRAMES MDF/HDF

Use a sublimation-ready picture frame that has a frame at least one inch wide. The larger the frame width, the better.

INGREDIENTS
☐ MDF/HDF picture frame
☐ Blowout paper (two sheets)
☐ Heat-resistant tape
☐ Sublimation transfer (print/sheet)

EQUIPMENT
☐ Lint roller
☐ Flat heat source such as a heat press
☐ Pen or pencil
☐ Ruler for placement help

PREPARATION

Pre-heat your flat heat press to the temperature shown in the chart below.

Remove the glass pane and frame backing.

Place your sublimation transfer face up on your work surface. **Lay the picture frame face down** on the sublimation transfer and align it where you'd like it to be. **Trace around both the inside and outside edges of the photo frame using a pen or pencil. Closely trim all of the edges** of your sublimation transfer.

Check to see if your photo frame has a protective film or cover. If so, remove it.

Use the lint roller to clean the surface of the photo frame.

Place a sheet of blowout paper (I recommend white cardstock or butcher paper) on your pressing pad, and **lay the picture frame face up** on top of it. Cover it with another piece of blowout paper and **pre-heat it for 5 seconds** to remove any moisture.

Place the sublimation transfer face down on the picture frame. Secure in place with heat-resistant tape.

Place a sheet of blowout paper (I recommend white cardstock or butcher paper) on your pressing pad.

Place the picture frame with the sublimation transfer on top on top of the blowout paper. Place another sheet of blowout paper on top.

Press according to the chart below. Pull the transfer sheet while still warm.

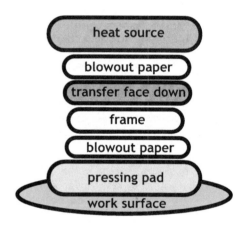

heat source
blowout paper
transfer face down
frame
blowout paper
pressing pad
work surface

COOK TIMES
Here are typical times you can use as a starting point. Always check the manufacturer's instructions for time and temperature, when available.

your favorite settings

Traditional Heat Press	AutoPress	EasyPress	Mini Press	
400°F / 204°C	400°F / 204°C	400°F / 204°C	High	
90 seconds	90 seconds	90 seconds	100 seconds	
40 psi (medium pressure)	Auto pressure	Medium pressure	Medium pressure	

TIPS & TRICKS
✗ Don't remove your sublimation transfer sheet for at least 10 seconds so it can cool down without ghosting.
✓ Remember that your sublimation design should be in the shape of a border.
✓ Once the frame has cooled, replace the glass pane, insert a photo, and replace the backing.

WALL SIGNS MDF/HDF

ALSO: Fiberboard signs, key hangers

MDF and HDF wall signs come in a variety of shapes and sizes. Some include hardware only on the back, while others have hardware on the front.

INGREDIENTS
☐ MDF/HDF wall sign blank
☐ Blowout paper (two sheets)
☐ Heat-resistant tape
☐ Sublimation transfer (print/sheet)

EQUIPMENT
☐ Lint roller
☐ Flat heat source such as a heat press
☐ (Optional) Ruler for placement help

PREPARATION

Pre-heat your flat heat press to the temperature shown in the chart below.

Closely trim the edges of your sublimation transfer.

Remove any hardware on the wall side and set it aside.

Check to see if your wall sign has a protective film or cover. If so, remove it.

Use the lint roller to clean the surface of the wall sign.

Place a sheet of blowout paper (I recommend white cardstock or butcher paper) on your pressing pad, and **lay the wall sign face up** on top of it. Cover it with another piece of blowout paper and **pre-heat it for 5 seconds** to remove any moisture.

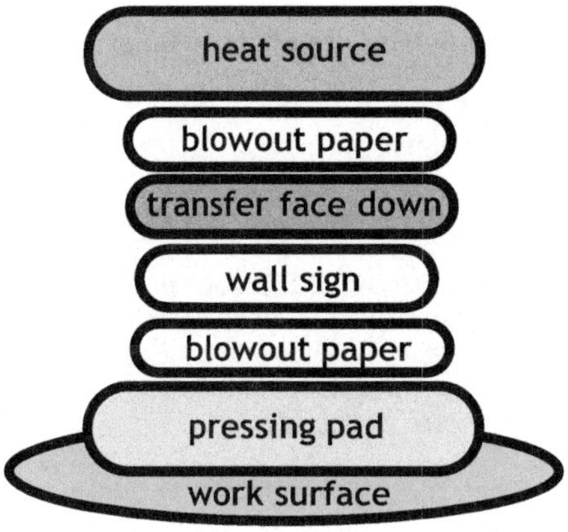

Place the sublimation transfer face down on the wall sign. Secure in place with heat-resistant tape.

Place a sheet of blowout paper (I recommend white cardstock or butcher paper) on your pressing pad.

Place the wall sign with the sublimation transfer on top of the blowout paper. Place another sheet of blowout paper on top.

Press according to the chart below. Pull the transfer sheet while still warm.

heat source
blowout paper
transfer face down
wall sign
blowout paper
pressing pad
work surface

COOK TIMES
Here are typical times you can use as a starting point. Always check the manufacturer's instructions for time and temperature, when available.

your favorite settings

Traditional Heat Press	AutoPress	EasyPress	Mini Press	
400°F / 204°C	400°F / 204°C	400°F / 204°C	High	
90 seconds	90 seconds	90 seconds	100 seconds	
40 psi (medium pressure)	Auto pressure	Medium pressure	Medium pressure	

TIPS & TRICKS
✗ Don't remove your sublimation transfer sheet for at least 10 seconds so it can cool down without ghosting.
✓ Remember to replace any hardware once the wall sign has cooled.

CLIPBOARDS MDF/HDF

ALSO: Dry erase boards

Clipboards come with hardware at the top. While it can sometimes successfully be removed and replaced, this is not always the case. It is best to avoid sublimating at the top near the hardware.

INGREDIENTS
☐ MDF/HDF Clipboard
☐ Blowout paper (two sheets)
☐ Heat-resistant tape
☐ Sublimation transfer (print/sheet)

EQUIPMENT
☐ Lint roller
☐ Flat heat source such as a heat press

PREPARATION

Pre-heat your flat heat press to the temperature shown in the chart below.

Closely trim the edges of your sublimation transfer.

Check to see if your clipboard has a protective film or cover. If so, remove it.

Use a lint roller to clean the surface of the clipboard.

Place a sheet of blowout paper (I recommend white cardstock or butcher paper) on your pressing pad, and **lay the clipboard face up** on top of it. Cover it with another piece of blowout paper and **pre-heat it for 5 seconds** to remove any moisture. Take care to avoid pressing the hardware at the top.

Place the blank side of the clipboard face up on your work surface. **Place your sublimation transfer face down** on top of the clipboard. The ink should be touching the blank face of the clipboard. Align and then **secure in place with heat-resistant tape.**

Place a sheet of blowout paper on the pressing pad. Next, **place the clipboard with the taped sublimation transfer side on top.** Place another sheet of blowout paper on top. Again, take care not to press the hardware at the top.

Press according to the chart below. Pull the transfer sheet while still warm.

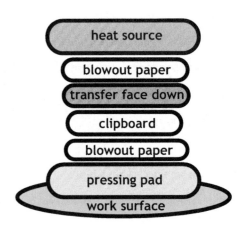

COOK TIMES
Here are typical times you can use as a starting point. Always check the manufacturer's instructions for time and temperature, when available.

your favorite settings

Traditional Heat Press	AutoPress	EasyPress	Mini Press	
400°F / 204°C	400°F / 204°C	400°F / 204°C	High	
70 seconds	70 seconds	70 seconds	80 seconds	
40 psi (medium pressure)	Auto pressure	Medium pressure	Medium pressure	

TIPS & TRICKS
✗ Don't remove your sublimation transfer sheet for at least 10 seconds so it can cool down without ghosting.
✓ If your clipboard hardware is not removable, let it hang just outside of the pressing area. Do not press the hardware.
✓ For a dry erase board tutorial check out *jennifermaker.com/Dollar-Tree-Sublimation-Ideas/*

MAGNETS MDF/HDF

Use a sublimation-ready MDF blank magnet to create custom magnets for your refrigerator, filing cabinet, magnetic dry-erase board, and more.

INGREDIENTS
☐ MDF/HDF magnet
☐ Blowout paper (two sheets)
☐ Heat-resistant tape
☐ Sublimation transfer (print/sheet)

EQUIPMENT
☐ Lint roller
☐ Flat heat source such as a heat press

PREPARATION

Pre-heat your flat heat press to the temperature shown in the chart below.

Closely trim the edges of your sublimation transfer.

Check to see if your magnet has a protective film or cover. If so, remove it.

Use a lint roller to clean the surface of the magnet.

Place a sheet of blowout paper (I recommend white cardstock or butcher paper) on your pressing pad, and **lay the magnet face up** on top of it. Cover it with another piece of blowout paper and **pre-heat it for 5 seconds** to remove any moisture.

Place the blank side of the magnet face up on your work surface. **Place your sublimation transfer face down** on top of the magnet. The ink should be touching the blank face of the magnet. Align and then **secure in place with heat-resistant tape.**

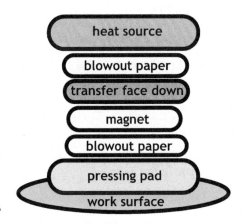

Place a sheet of blowout paper on the pressing pad. Next, **place the magnet with the taped sublimation transfer side on top.** Place another sheet of blowout paper on top.

Press according to the chart below. Pull the transfer sheet while still warm.

COOK TIMES
Here are typical times you can use as a starting point. Always check the manufacturer's instructions for time and temperature, when available.

your favorite settings

Traditional Heat Press	AutoPress	EasyPress	Mini Press	
365°F / 185°C	365°F / 185°C	360°F / 183°F	High	
55 seconds	55 seconds	55 seconds	60 seconds	
30 psi (light pressure)	Auto pressure	Light pressure	Light pressure	

TIPS & TRICKS
× Don't remove your sublimation transfer sheet for at least 10 seconds so it can cool down without ghosting.
× If your MDF or hardboard blanks are yellowing after pressing, try lowering the heat or pressing time.
✓ Many sublimation magnets come with the actual magnet separated from the MDF or hardboard blank. If this is the case for you, remember to just peel the backing off of the magnet and attach it to the back of your blank after you have pressed it.

PUZZLES MDF/HDF

Create your own puzzles is varying sizes using sublimation-ready MDF/HDF blanks. Because MDF and HDF are sturdier than cardboard, these puzzles will be great for children.

INGREDIENTS
☐ Puzzle blank
☐ Blowout paper (two sheets)
☐ Heat-resistant tape
☐ Sublimation transfer (print/sheet)

EQUIPMENT
☐ Lint roller
☐ Flat heat source such as a heat press

PREPARATION

Pre-heat your flat heat press to the temperature shown in the chart below.

Closely trim the edges of your sublimation transfer.

Use the lint roller to clean the surface of the puzzle.

Place a sheet of blowout paper (I recommend white cardstock or butcher paper) on your pressing pad, and **lay the puzzle face up** on top of it. Cover it with another piece of blowout paper and **pre-heat it for 5 seconds** to remove any moisture.

Place the sublimation transfer face down on the puzzle. Secure in place with heat-resistant tape.

Place a sheet of blowout paper on your pressing pad.

Place the puzzle with the sublimation transfer on top of the blowout paper. Place another sheet of blowout paper on top.

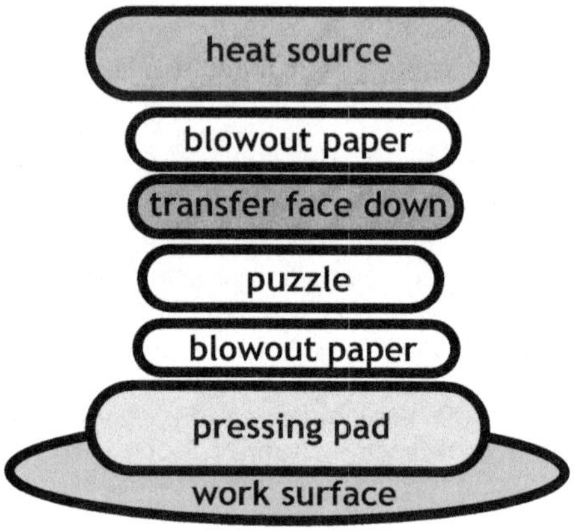

Press according to the chart below. Pull the transfer sheet while still warm.

heat source
blowout paper
transfer face down
puzzle
blowout paper
pressing pad
work surface

COOK TIMES
Here are typical times you can use as a starting point. Always check the manufacturer's instructions for time and temperature, when available.

your favorite settings

Traditional Heat Press	AutoPress	EasyPress	Mini Press	
365°F / 185°C	375°F / 190°C	365°F / 185°C	High	
60 seconds	60 seconds	60 seconds	75 seconds	
30 psi (light pressure)	Auto pressure	Light pressure	Light pressure	

TIPS & TRICKS
✗ Don't remove your sublimation transfer sheet for at least 10 seconds so it can cool down without ghosting.
✓ If your puzzle comes with a backing piece of cardboard, keep it with the puzzle when pressing. This will help keep the pieces of the puzzle in place.

TAGS MDF/HDF

ALSO: Ornaments

Use a sublimation-ready MDF or HDF blank to create a customized luggage tag, bag tag, or key tag. These blanks come in a variety of shapes and sizes.

INGREDIENTS
- ☐ MDF tag (any shape)
- ☐ Blowout paper (two sheets)
- ☐ Heat-resistant tape
- ☐ Sublimation transfer (print/sheet)

EQUIPMENT
- ☐ Lint roller
- ☐ Flat heat source such as a heat press

PREPARATION

Pre-heat your flat heat press to the temperature shown in the chart below.

Closely trim the edges of your sublimation transfer.

If your tag comes with a hanger of any kind (chain, plastic, clip, ribbon, etc.) temporarily remove it and set it aside. **Check to see if there is a protective film or cover.** If so, remove it. Remember to check both sides of the tag.

Use the lint roller to clean the surface of the tag.

Place a sheet of blowout paper (I recommend white cardstock or butcher paper) on your pressing pad, and **lay the tag face up** on top of it. Cover it with another piece of blowout paper and **pre-heat it for 5 seconds** to remove any moisture.

Place the sublimation transfer face up on your work surface. **Lay the tag face down** on top of the sublimation transfer and align it. **Secure it in place with heat-resistant tape.**

Place a sheet of blowout paper on the pressing pad. Next, **place the tag with the taped sublimation transfer facing up.** Place another sheet of blowout paper on top.

Press according to the chart below. Pull the transfer sheet while still warm.

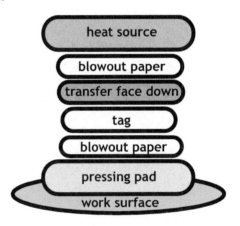

heat source
blowout paper
transfer face down
tag
blowout paper
pressing pad
work surface

COOK TIMES
Here are typical times you can use as a starting point. Always check the manufacturer's instructions for time and temperature, when available.

your favorite settings

Traditional Heat Press	AutoPress	EasyPress	Mini Press	
365°F / 185°C	375°F / 190°C	365°F / 185°C	High	
55 seconds	60 seconds	55 seconds	60 seconds	
30 psi (light pressure)	Auto pressure	Light pressure	Light pressure	

TIPS & TRICKS
× Don't remove your sublimation transfer sheet for at least 10 seconds so it can cool down without ghosting.
✓ Remember to mirror your design, otherwise, your text and image will be backward.

CHAPTER 5
GLASS

CUTTING BOARDS GLASS

ALSO: Cheese board, charcuterie tray, stained glass cutting board

Sublimatable glass cutting boards can make a beautiful decorative piece, cheese board, or charcuterie tray. Many glass cutting boards have a textured surface on the front and a smooth surface on the back.

INGREDIENTS
☐ Heat resistant glass cutting board
☐ Blowout paper (two sheets)
☐ Heat-resistant tape
☐ Sublimation transfer (print/sheet)

EQUIPMENT
☐ Lint-free cloth
☐ Rubbing alcohol
☐ Flat heat source such as a heat press
☐ Cricut spatula (to remove rubber feet)

PREPARATION

Pre-heat your flat heat press to the temperature shown in the chart below.

Closely trim the edges of your printed sublimation transfer so that it is 1/4 inch larger than the cutting board.

Temporarily remove the rubber feet on the glass cutting board. Set them aside for later.

Clean both sides of the sublimation blank with with rubbing alcohol and a lint-free cloth.

Lay the cutting board with the smooth side up on your work surface. **Secure the sublimation transfer face down** on the cutting board using heat-resistant tape.

Place a piece of blowout paper on the pressing pad (I recommend white cardstock or butcher paper). **Place the cutting board with the smooth side** (the side with the sublimation transfer) face up.

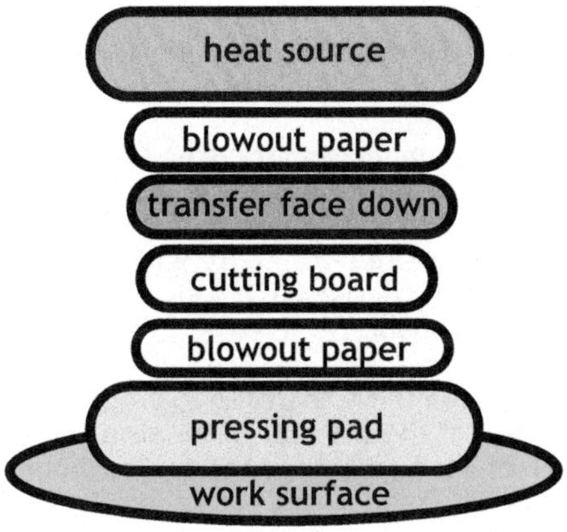

Cover with another sheet of blowout paper.

Press according to the chart below. Pull the transfer sheet while still warm.

heat source
blowout paper
transfer face down
cutting board
blowout paper
pressing pad
work surface

COOK TIMES
Here are typical times you can use as a starting point. Always check the manufacturer's instructions for time and temperature, when available.

your favorite settings

Traditional Heat Press	AutoPress	EasyPress	Mini Press	
385°F / 196°C	385°F / 196°C	385°F / 196°C	High	
190 seconds	190 seconds	190 seconds	200 seconds	
40 psi (medium pressure)	Auto pressure	Medium pressure	Medium pressure	

TIPS & TRICKS
✗ Don't remove your sublimation transfer sheet for at least 10 seconds so it can cool down without ghosting.
✓ Try to press your whole design at the same time. If you have separate designs and press them separately, you risk re-sublimating the ink already applied, which could cause ghosting or blurring.
✓ Remember to replace the rubber feet on the smooth side of your cutting board once it has cooled.
✓ For a tutorial check out jennifermaker.com/Dollar-Tree-Sublimation-Ideas/
✓ For a stained glass cutting board tutorial go to: https://www.jennifermaker.com/can-you-sublimate-on-glass/

DRINKWARE (HANDLE) GLASS

ALSO: Glass steins, Mason jars, beer mugs, coffee mugs

Sublimatable glass drinkware with handles come in many commonly available sizes and varieties, including steins, mason jars, and mugs.

INGREDIENTS
☐ Heat resistant drinkware glass of your choice
☐ Blowout paper (one sheet)
☐ Heat-resistant tape
☐ Sublimation transfer (print/sheet)

EQUIPMENT
☐ Lint-free cloth
☐ Rubbing alcohol
☐ Heat source appropriate for drinkware

PREPARATION

Pre-heat your heat press to the temperature shown in the chart below.

Use a lint-free cloth and rubbing alcohol to clean the glass drinkware.

Trim all four edges of the sublimation transfer so that no white edges are visible.

Wrap the sublimation transfer around the glass drinkware so the ink touches the surface. How much of the drinkware is covered depends on whether your design is only on one side or from handle-to-handle. For a full-coverage design, **place the drinkware with the handle facing you** and place the center of the design on the opposite side, smoothing each side as it moves toward the handle.

Firmly tape the transfer to itself underneath the handle. Then, secure the rest of the transfer to the drinkware by applying heat-resistant tape to each of the edges. **Tape the top, bottom, left, and right edges** as though following directions on a compass. **Rotate the drinkware slightly** and repeat until the design transfer is completely covered. The edges of the tape should fold over into the drinkware at the top, as well as onto the bottom of the drinkware.

Use a scraper to thoroughly work air pockets out.

Wrap the drinkware in a piece of butcher paper, securing it with tape.

Press according to the chart below. Pull the transfer sheet while still warm.

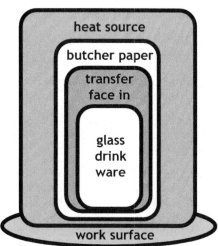

COOK TIMES
Here are typical times you can use as a starting point. Always check the manufacturer's instructions for time and temperature, when available.

your favorite settings

Tumbler Press	Convection Oven	Air Fryer	
385°F / 196°C	400°F / 204°C	400°F / 204°C	
120-240 seconds	8 minutes	8 minutes	
40 psi (medium pressure)			

TIPS & TRICKS
✓ Turn your drinkware 180 degrees halfway through the cooking time.
✗ Don't remove your sublimation transfer sheet for at least 10 seconds so it can cool down without ghosting.
✓ Always use heat-resistant gloves when placing/removing your drinkware in/from the heat source.

DRINKWARE (NO HANDLE) GLASS

ALSO: Glass bottles, Mason jars, cans, cups, water bottles

Sublimatable glass drinkware with no handles comes in many commonly available sizes and varieties, including bottles, mason jars, and cans.

INGREDIENTS
☐ Heat resistant drinkware glass of your choice
☐ Blowout paper (one sheet)
☐ Heat-resistant tape
☐ Sublimation transfer (print/sheet)

EQUIPMENT
☐ Lint-free cloth
☐ Rubbing alcohol
☐ Heat source appropriate for drinkware

PREPARATION

Pre-heat your heat press to the temperature shown in the chart below.

Use a lint-free cloth and rubbing alcohol to clean the glass drinkware.

Trim the top, bottom, and right edges of the sublimation transfer at the edge of the ink so that no white edges are visible. Trim the left edge to leave a quarter inch strip of white.

Wrap the sublimation transfer around the glass drinkware so the ink touches the surface. The transfer should overlap slightly, with the quarter inch strip of white on top. **Firmly tape the transfer to itself, then tape along the seam,** leaving an inch or so untaped along the top and bottom.

Press hard and smooth the paper from both sides toward the seam. If anything ripples, remove tape and try again. **Add tape to cover the top and bottom remainders of your seam,** allowing some of the tape to fold over the top and bottom edges. Use a scraper to thoroughly work air pockets out.

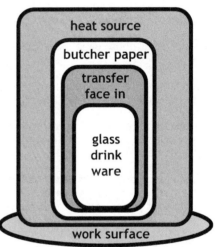

Firmly tape the transfer along all the top and bottom edges of the drinkware. **Tape the top, bottom, left, and right edges** as though following directions on a compass. **Rotate the drinkware slightly** and repeat until the design transfer is completely covered. The edges of the tape should fold over into the drinkware at the top, as well as onto the bottom of the drinkware.

Wrap the drinkware in a piece of butcher paper, securing it with tape.

Press according to the chart below. Pull the transfer sheet while still warm.

COOK TIMES
Here are typical times you can use as a starting point. Always check the manufacturer's instructions for time and temperature, when available.

your favorite settings

Tumbler Press	Convection Oven	Air Fryer	
385°F / 196°C	400°F / 204°C	400°F / 204°C	
120-240 seconds	8 minutes	8 minutes	
40 psi (medium pressure)			

TIPS & TRICKS
✓ Turn your drinkware 180 degrees halfway through the cooking time.
✗ Don't remove your sublimation transfer sheet for at least 10 seconds so it can cool down without ghosting.
✓ For a tutorial check out jennifermaker.com/cricut-mug-press-sublimation-blanks/

TILES & PHOTO PANELS GLASS

Check to see if the sublimation coating is on the front or back of your glass tile or photo panel. If it is on the front, you will need to mirror your design.

INGREDIENTS
☐ Heat resistant glass tile
☐ Blowout paper (two sheets)
☐ Heat-resistant tape
☐ Sublimation transfer (print/sheet)

EQUIPMENT
☐ Lint-free cloth
☐ Rubbing alcohol
☐ Flat heat source such as a heat press

PREPARATION

Pre-heat your flat heat press to the temperature shown in the chart below.

Closely trim the edges of your printed sublimation transfer.

If your tile or photo panel has rubber feet attached, remove them for now.

Clean the tile or photo panel with rubbing alcohol and a lint-free cloth. This should be the side with the sublimation coating.

Lay the tile or photo panel with the sublimation-ready side up on your work surface. Secure the sublimation transfer face down on the tile using heat-resistant tape.

Place a piece of blowout paper on the pressing pad (I recommend white cardstock or butcher paper). **Place the tile or photo panel on the blowout paper with the sublimation transfer face up.**

Cover with another sheet of blowout paper.

Press according to the chart below. Pull the transfer sheet while still warm.

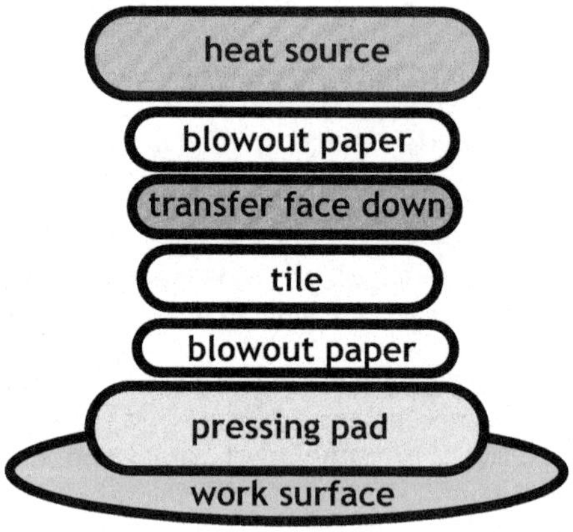

heat source
blowout paper
transfer face down
tile
blowout paper
pressing pad
work surface

COOK TIMES
Here are typical times you can use as a starting point. Always check the manufacturer's instructions for time and temperature, when available.

your favorite settings

Traditional Heat Press	AutoPress	EasyPress	Mini Press	
385°F / 196°C	385°F / 196°C	385°F / 196°C	High	
190 seconds	190 seconds	190 seconds	200 seconds	
40 psi (medium pressure)	Auto pressure	Medium pressure	Medium pressure	

TIPS & TRICKS
✗ Don't remove your sublimation transfer sheet for at least 10 seconds so it can cool down without ghosting.
✓ If your tile comes with rubber feet, attach them to the sublimated side of the tile once it has cooled.
✓ If your photo panel comes with a standing peg, wait until it has cooled to attach it.

ORNAMENTS GLASS

Sublimatable glass ornaments are made with either a flat or beveled surface and usually come in simple shapes.

INGREDIENTS
☐ Heat resistant flat glass ornament
☐ Blowout paper (two sheets)
☐ Heat-resistant tape
☐ Sublimation transfer (print/sheet)

EQUIPMENT
☐ Lint-free cloth
☐ Rubbing alcohol
☐ Flat heat source such as a heat press

PREPARATION

Pre-heat your flat heat press to the temperature shown in the chart below.

Closely trim the edges of your printed sublimation transfer.

Temporarily remove the ribbon or other hanger from the ornament.

Clean the ornament with rubbing alcohol and a lint-free cloth. This should be the side with the sublimation coating.

Lay the ornament with the sublimation-ready side up on your work surface. Secure the sublimation transfer face down on the ornament using heat-resistant tape.

Place a piece of blowout paper on the pressing pad (I recommend white cardstock or butcher paper). **Place the ornament with** the sublimation transfer face up onto the blowout paper.

Cover with another sheet of blowout paper.

Press according to the chart below. Pull the transfer sheet while still warm.

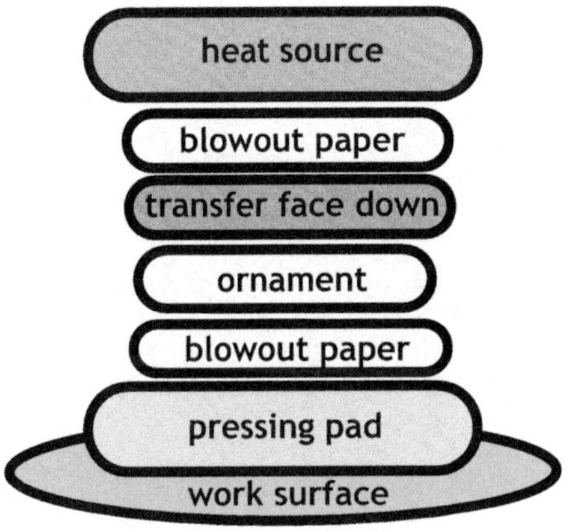

heat source
blowout paper
transfer face down
ornament
blowout paper
pressing pad
work surface

COOK TIMES
Here are typical times you can use as a starting point. Always check the manufacturer's instructions for time and temperature, when available.

your favorite settings

Traditional Heat Press	AutoPress	EasyPress	Mini Press	
400°F / 204°C	400°F / 204°C	400°F / 204°C	High	
90 seconds	90 seconds	90 seconds	100 seconds	
40 psi (Medium pressure)	Auto pressure	Medium pressure	Medium pressure	

TIPS & TRICKS
✗ Don't remove your sublimation transfer sheet for at least 10 seconds so it can cool down without ghosting.
✓ Remember to reattach the ribbon or other hanger to your ornament once it has cooled.
✓ For a tutorial check out jennifermaker.com/diy-sublimation-ornaments/

CHAPTER 6
SLATE

PHOTO SLATE SLATE

Create a beautiful photo keepsake using a sublimation-ready photo slate. These come in different shapes and sizes, but this recipe is specifically for square and rectangular shapes.

INGREDIENTS
☐ Blank square or rectangular photo slate
☐ Blowout paper (two sheets)
☐ Heat-resistant tape
☐ Sublimation transfer (print/sheet)

EQUIPMENT
☐ Lint roller
☐ Flat heat source such as a heat press
☐ Heat conductive green rubber pad
☐ Heat resistant gloves
☐ Cooling rack

PREPARATION

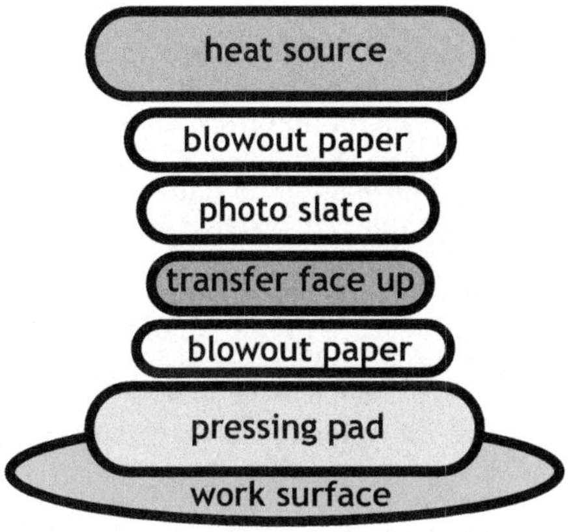

Start with a new photo slate for the best results.

Pre-heat your flat heat press to the temperature shown in the chart below.

Trim the edges of your printed sublimation transfer.

Use the lint roller to clean the surface of your photo slate.

Lay the photo slate face-up on your work surface. Place the sublimation transfer face down on the slate. **Secure it in place with heat-resistant tape.**

Lay a sheet of blowout paper on the pressing pad.

Place your photo slate face down on the blowout paper. The sublimation transfer should be underneath the slate.

Lay another sheet of blowout paper on top of the photo slate. Place the heat conductive green rubber pad on top of everything. Make sure it covers the slate complately.

Press according to the chart below. Using heat resisant gloves pull the transfer sheet while still warm. Place the slate on a cooling rack.

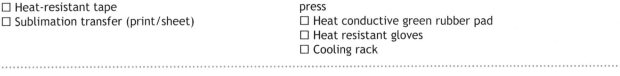

COOK TIMES
Here are typical times you can use as a starting point. Always check the manufacturer's instructions for time and temperature, when available.

your favorite settings

Traditional Heat Press	AutoPress	EasyPress	Mini Press	
400°F / 204°C	400°F / 204°C	400°F / 204°C	High	
420-450 seconds	420 seconds	420 seconds	450 seconds	
50 psi (heavy pressure)	Auto pressure	Heavy pressure	Heavy pressure	

TIPS & TRICKS
✓ Remember to mirror your design, especially if it has text.
✗ Don't remove your sublimation transfer sheet for at least 10 seconds so it can cool down without ghosting.
✓ If you are using a traditional heat press, be sure to adjust the pressure before turning the heat press on.
✓ A traditional heat press is easiest for pressing slate due to the pressure needed, but an EasyPress works as long as you are physically capable of maintaining the pressure for the length of time required.

NON-SQUARE SLATE SLATE

Create a beautiful photo keepsake using a sublimation-ready photo slate. These come in different shapes and sizes, but this recipe is specifically for non-square shapes, such as circles, ovals, hearts, and more.

INGREDIENTS
☐ Non-square photo slate
☐ Blowout paper (two sheets)
☐ Heat-resistant tape
☐ Sublimation transfer (print/sheet)

EQUIPMENT
☐ Lint roller
☐ Flat heat source such as a heat press
☐ Heat resistant gloves
☐ Cooling rack
☐ Heat conductive green rubber pad
☐ Pencil and Ruler

PREPARATION

Start with a new photo slate for the best results.

Pre-heat your flat heat press to the temperature shown in the chart below.

Lay your sublimation transfer face up and place your sublimation transfer face up on top of it. Place it over the area of the transfer that you'd like on your photo slate. Trace around the photo slate with a pencil. Remember that you will lose a little bit around each edge.

Trim your printed sublimation transfer to match the shape of your photo slate, taking care to note where the widest and narrowest points fall. You don't want to accidentally exclude any important parts.

Use the lint roller to clean the surface of your photo slate.

Lay the photo slate face-up on your work surface. **Place the sublimation transfer face down** on the slate. Secure it in place with heat-resistant tape.

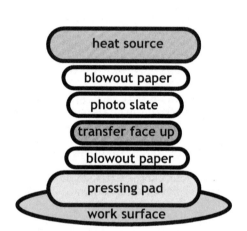

Lay a sheet of blowout paper on the pressing pad.

Place your photo slate face down on the blowout paper. The sublimation transfer should be underneath the slate. Lay another sheet of blowout paper on top of the photo slate. Place the heat conductive green rubber pad on top of everything. Make sure it covers the slate complately.

Press according to the chart below. Using heat resisant gloves pull the transfer sheet while still warm and place the slate on a cooling rack.

COOK TIMES
Here are typical times you can use as a starting point. Always check the manufacturer's instructions for time and temperature, when available.

your favorite settings

Traditional Heat Press	Auto Press	Easy Press	Mini Press		
400°F / 204°C	400°F / 204°C	400°F / 204°C	High		
420-450 seconds	420 seconds	420 seconds	450 seconds		
50 psi (heavy pressure)	Auto pressure	Heavy pressure	Heavy pressure		

TIPS & TRICKS
✓ Remember to mirror your design, especially if it has text.
✗ Don't remove your sublimation transfer sheet for at least 10 seconds so it can cool down without ghosting.
✓ If you are using a traditional heat press, be sure to adjust the pressure before turning the heat press on.

CHAPTER 7
ALUMINUM

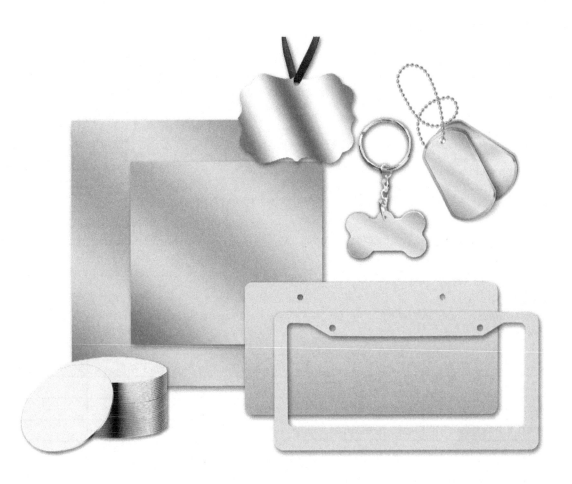

PHOTO PANELS ALUMINUM

This recipe is for any size aluminum photo panel. The sublimatable photo panels come in various finishes including matte white, glossy white, matte clear, and glossy clear.

INGREDIENTS
☐ Aluminum sublimation photo panel
☐ Blowout paper (two sheets)
☐ Heat-resistant tape
☐ Sublimation transfer (print/sheet)

EQUIPMENT
☐ Lint roller
☐ Flat heat source such as a heat press
☐ Microfiber cloth

PREPARATION

Start with a blank sublimation aluminum photo panel.

Pre-heat your flat heat press to the temperature shown in the chart below.

You will want your **sublimation transfer sized a little larger than the photo panel** to avoid ghosting and to have the image cover the photo panel.

Peel the protective film from the photo panel.

Position the sublimation transfer directly onto the photo panel (same side that you removed the film) and secure it with heat-resistant tape.

Place the photo panel with the sublimation transfer side down on a piece of blowout paper (I recommend white cardstock or butcher paper) onto your pressing pad.

Place a piece of **blowout paper** on top of the back side of the photo panel.

Press the photo panel for the time indicated below.

The aluminum sheet will be very hot. **Wear heat protective gloves** to handle it after sublimation.

Allow to cool before removing the sublimation transfer.

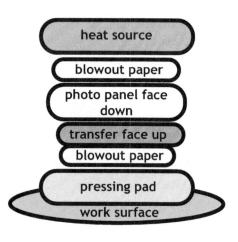

heat source
blowout paper
photo panel face down
transfer face up
blowout paper
pressing pad
work surface

COOK TIMES
Here are typical times you can use as a starting point. Always check the manufacturer's instructions for time and temperature, when available.

your favorite settings

Traditional Heat Press	AutoPress	EasyPress	Mini Press	
400°F / 204°C	385°F / 196°C	360°F / 192°C	High	
60 seconds	50 seconds	120 seconds	70 seconds	
40 psi (medium pressure)	Auto pressure	Light pressure	Light pressure	

TIPS & TRICKS
✗ Don't remove your sublimation transfer sheet for at least 10 seconds so it can cool down without ghosting.
✓ If the sublimation print is smaller than the photo panel, then trim the print at the edge of the image.
✓ If you removed the plastic film previously, use a microfiber cloth or lens wipe to remove dust and debris.
✓ After Care: To wash, use a microfiber cloth to remove fingerprints and dust. A small amount of alcohol may help if the photo print gets dirty.

LICENSE PLATES ALUMINUM

ALSO: Mini license plate, Mini street signs, and general signs

This recipe is for sublimatable aluminum license plates. This process can also be applied to sublimation aluminum mini street signs, and sublimation aluminum signs.

INGREDIENTS
☐ Sublimation blank
☐ Blow-out paper (two sheets)
☐ Heat-resistant tape
☐ Sublimation transfer (print/sheet)

EQUIPMENT
☐ Flat heat source such as a heat press

PREPARATION

Start with a blank sublimation license plate.

Pre-heat your flat heat press to the temperature shown in the chart below.

Remove the clear plastic protective film on the sublimation side of the license plate frame.

Place your license plate frame on a piece of blowout paper with the sublimation side facing up.

Double-check your sublimation transfer. For exampe, if you have words on your image, you want to make sure that your image is mirrored.

Trim your sublimation transfer sheet. You will want to ensure that the image extends beyond the license plate's edge. This will allow the image to sublimate to the edge of the plate without leaving a line around the edge.

Align your **sublimation transfer** and secure with heat-resistant tape. Make sure to tape all four edges of the transfer to ensure that it stays in place during pressing.

Cover the entire license plate with blowout paper.

Press the license plate for the time indicated below.

The aluminum will be very hot, **wear heat-resistant gloves** to handle after sublimation.

Allow to cool before removing the sublimation transfer.

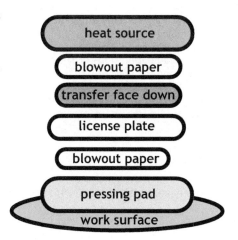

COOK TIMES
Here are typical times you can use as a starting point. Always check the manufacturer's instructions for time and temperature, when available.

your favorite settings

Traditional Heat Press	AutoPress	EasyPress	Mini Press	
400°F / 204°C	385°F / 196°C	360°F / 192°C	High	
60 seconds	50 seconds	120 seconds	70 seconds	
40 psi (medium pressure)	Auto pressure	Light pressure	Light pressure	

TIPS & TRICKS
✗ Don't remove your sublimation transfer sheet for at least 10 seconds so it can cool down without ghosting.

LICENSE PLATE FRAMES
ALUMINUM

This recipe is for an aluminum sublimation-ready license plate frame. These frames can be purchased with either a white gloss base or a chrome base.

INGREDIENTS
☐ Sublimation license plate frame
☐ Blowout Paper (Two Sheets)
☐ Heat-resistant tape
☐ Sublimation transfer (Print/Sheet)

EQUIPMENT
☐ Flat heat source such as a heat press

PREPARATION

Start with a blank sublimation license plate frame.

Pre-heat your flat heat press to the temperature shown in the chart below.

Remove the clear plastic protective film on the sublimation side of the license plate frame.

Place your license plate frame on a piece of blowout paper with the sublimation side facing up.

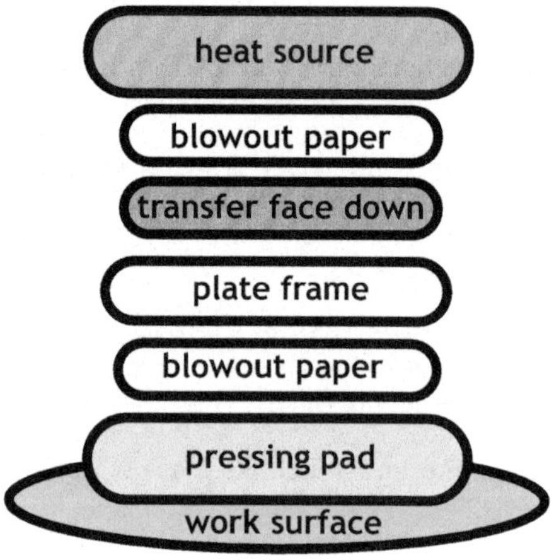

Double-check your sublimation transfer. If you have words, make sure you mirror the image before printing.

Trim your sublimation transfer sheet. You will want to ensure that the image extends beyond the edge of the license plate frame. This will allow the image to sublimate to the edge of the frame without leaving a line around the edge.

Align your **sublimation transfer** and secure with heat-resistant tape. Make sure to tape all four edges of the transfer to ensure that it stays in place during pressing.

Cover the entire license plate frame with blowout paper.

Press the license plate frame for the time indicated below.

The license plate frame will be very hot. **Wear heat-resistant gloves** to handle after sublimation.

Allow to cool before removing the sublimation transfer.

heat source
blowout paper
transfer face down
plate frame
blowout paper
pressing pad
work surface

COOK TIMES
Here are typical times you can use as a starting point. Always check the manufacturer's instructions for time and temperature, when available.

your favorite settings

Traditional Heat Press	AutoPress	EasyPress	Mini Press	
400°F / 204°C	385°F / 196°C	360°F / 192°C	High	
60 seconds	50 seconds	120 seconds	70 seconds	
40 psi (medium pressure)	Auto pressure	Light pressure	Light pressure	

TIPS & TRICKS
✗ Don't remove your sublimation transfer sheet for at least 10 seconds so it can cool down without ghosting.
✓ To ensure the longevity of your image, you can use UV-protected sublimation ink or spray the finished product with a UV-protecting spray.

BUSINESS CARDS ALUMINUM
ALSO: Aluminum name badge, phone case inserts

This recipe is for sublimation-ready aluminum business card blanks.

INGREDIENTS
☐ Sublimation blank aluminum business cards
☐ Blowout paper (two sheets)
☐ Heat-resistant tape
☐ Sublimation transfer (print/sheet)

EQUIPMENT
☐ Flat heat source such as a heat press

PREPARATION

Start with a new aluminum sublimation business card blank. You can sublimate multiple blanks at one time.

Pre-heat your flat heat press to the temperature shown in the chart below.

Trim your sublimation transfer sheet. You will want to ensure that the image extends beyond the edge of the business card(s), ideally a quarter-inch or larger. This will allow the image to sublimate to the edge of the card without leaving a line around the edge.

Remove the clear plastic protective film on both sides of the business card blank.

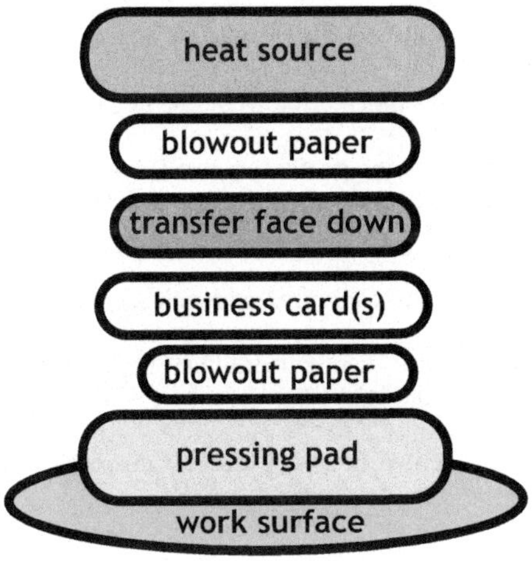

Place a **piece of blowout paper (I recommend white cardstock or butcher paper)** on your pressing pad.

You can **sublimate both sides of the business card(s).** If you are sublimating both sides of the card(s), place the sublimation transfer sheet for the back of the business card face-up on the blowout paper. Then place the business card(s) on top of the transfer sheet.

If you are only **sublimating one side of the business card(s)** place the business card(s) on top of the blowout paper.

Carefully align and place the top sublimation transfer sheet face down on each of the business cards.

Tape all four edges of the top sublimation transfer sheet(s) face down. **Cover all of the business cards** with blowout paper.

Press the business cards for the time indicated below. **Allow to cool** before removing the transfer sheet.

heat source

blowout paper

transfer face down

business card(s)

blowout paper

pressing pad

work surface

COOK TIMES
Here are typical times you can use as a starting point. Always check the manufacturer's instructions for time and temperature, when available.

your favorite settings

Traditional Heat Press	AutoPress	EasyPress	Mini Press	
400°F / 204°C	385°F / 196°C	360°F / 192°C	High	
60 seconds	50 seconds	120 seconds	70 seconds	
40 psi (medium pressure)	Auto pressure	Light pressure	Light pressure	

TIPS & TRICKS
✗ Allow the product to cool before removing the sublimation transfer sheet, aluminum will get very hot.
✓ After Care: Use a microfiber cloth to remove fingerprints and dust.
✓ If your blank is a phone case insert, allow to cool before inserting it into the plastic phone case.

STICKERS ALUMINUM

ALSO: Phone grip decals, circle pendants, ID tags

This recipe is for an aluminum sublimation blank that can be attached to an adhesive to create a decal or sticker.

INGREDIENTS
☐ Small aluminum sublimation blank
☐ Blowout paper (two sheets)
☐ Heat-resistant tape
☐ Sublimation transfer (print/sheet)
☐ Double-sided adhesive for stickers

EQUIPMENT
☐ Flat heat source such as a heat press
☐ Microfiber cloth

PREPARATION

Start with a new aluminum sublimation blank.

Pre-heat your flat heat press to the temperature shown in the chart below.

Trim your sublimation transfer sheet. You will want to ensure that the image extends just beyond the edge of the sublimation blank. This will allow the image to sublimate to the edge without leaving a line around the edge or ghosting.

Place a piece of blowout paper on your pressing pad.

Remove the protective film from your sublimation blank. If there is no film or it was removed previously, use a piece of microfiber cloth to wipe away any dust or debris.

Place your sublimation blank sublimation side up on the blowout paper.

Carefully **align your sublimation transfer sheet** face-side down onto the sublimation blank.

Using **heat-resistant tape** secure your design to the sublimation blank.

Place a piece of blowout paper on top of the sublimation transfer sheet.

Press according to the chart below.

Allow to cool, and carefully remove the transfer paper using heat-resistant gloves.

If you are creating a sticker, apply the double-sided adhesive to the back of the sublimation blank after allowing the product to cool completely.

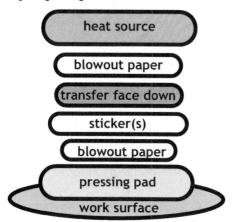

COOK TIMES
Here are typical times you can use as a starting point. Always check the manufacturer's instructions for time and temperature, when available.

your favorite settings

Traditional Heat Press	AutoPress	EasyPress	Mini Press	
400°F / 204°C	385°F / 196°C	360°F / 192°C	High	
60 seconds	50 seconds	120 seconds	70 seconds	
40 psi (medium pressure)	Auto pressure	Light pressure	Light pressure	

TIPS & TRICKS
✗ Aluminum will be very hot after pressing, so always use heat-resistant gloves to help prevent burns.
✓ For some of the blanks, you are able to sublimate on both sides. You can do this at the same time with two transfer sheets.
✓ After Care: Using a microfiber cloth after sublimation can help remove fingerprints and dust.

ORNAMENTS ALUMINUM

ALSO: Two-sided ornaments, pendants, dog tags

This recipe is for aluminum sublimation ornament blanks, one or two-sided.

INGREDIENTS
☐ One or two sided sublimation blank
☐ Blowout paper (two sheets)
☐ Heat-resistant tape
☐ Sublimation transfer (print/sheet)

EQUIPMENT
☐ Flat heat source such as a heat press

PREPARATION

Start with a new sublimation blank. Then, choose between one-sided or two-sided ornament blanks.

Remove the plastic film from the blank's sublimation side(s).

Pre-heat your flat heat press to the temperature shown in the chart below.

Trim the edges of your printed sublimation transfer, leaving a quarter of an inch to extend around the edges of the ornament.

Place a piece of **blowout paper** (I recommend white cardstock or butcher paper) on your pressing pad.

If you are **sublimating both sides,** you will make a sandwich with the transfer sheets and the ornament in the middle. Place one of the transfer sheets down directly on the bottom blowout paper. Transfer side face up.

Place the ornament with the sublimation side up on the blowout paper.

Align the sublimation transfer face-side down on top of the ornament.

Tape all four edges of your design down to the blowout paper to help prevent ghosting or the image shifting during pressing. If sublimating both sides of the ornament, place and tape the transfer on the other side in the same manner.

Cover with another piece of blowout paper.

Press according to the chart below.

Allow to cool, and then using **heat-resistant gloves,** remove the sublimation transfer sheet.

| heat source |
| blowout paper |
| transfer face down |
| ornament(s) |
| transfer face up* |
| blowout paper |
| pressing pad |
| work surface |

* optional

COOK TIMES
Here are typical times you can use as a starting point. Always check the manufacturer's instructions for time and temperature, when available.

your favorite settings

Traditional Heat Press	AutoPress	EasyPress	Mini Press	
400°F / 204°C	385°F / 196°C	360°F / 192°C	High	
75 seconds	60 seconds	120 seconds	70 seconds	
40 psi (medium)	Auto pressure	Light pressure	Light pressure	

TIPS & TRICKS
✗ Don't remove your sublimation transfer sheet for at least 10 seconds so it can cool down without ghosting.
✓ For a tutorial check out jennifermaker.com/diy-sublimation-ornaments/

WIND SPINNERS ALUMINUM

This recipe is for a double-sided aluminum sublimation wind spinner blanks, these come in a variety of shapes and sizes.

INGREDIENTS
☐ Wind spinner sublimation blank
☐ Blowout paper (two sheets)
☐ Heat-resistant tape
☐ Sublimation transfer (print/sheet)

EQUIPMENT
☐ Flat heat source such as a heat press

PREPARATION

Start with a new sublimation blank.

Remove the plastic film from the blank's sublimation side(s).

Pre-heat your flat heat press to the temperature shown in the chart below.

Align your sublimation transfer so that the focal point is within the center shape of the sublimation blank.

Using heat-resistant tape secure the sublimation transfer to the blank.

Place a piece of **blowout paper** (I recommend white cardstock or butcher paper) on your pressing pad.

You will sublimate one side at a time.

Place the wind spinner with the sublimation side up on the blowout paper.

Cover with another piece of blowout paper.

Press according to the chart below.

Allow to cool, and then using **heat-resistant gloves**, remove the sublimation transfer sheet.

Repeat the steps for the 2nd side of the wind spinner.

| heat source |
| blowout paper |
| transfer face down |
| wind spinner |
| blowout paper |
| pressing pad |
| work surface |

COOK TIMES
Here are typical times you can use as a starting point. Always check the manufacturer's instructions for time and temperature, when available.

your favorite settings

Traditional Heat Press	AutoPress	EasyPress	Mini Press	
385°F / 196°C	385°F / 196°C	360°F / 192°C	High	
60 seconds	60 seconds	120 seconds	70 seconds	
40 psi (medium)	Auto pressure	Light pressure	Light pressure	

TIPS & TRICKS
✗ Don't remove your sublimation transfer sheet for at least 10 seconds so it can cool down without ghosting.
✓ Make sure to remove the protective cover from both sides of the sublimation blank before pressing.
✓ When aligning the second transfer sheet you can use the design on the sublimation blank to align with the print.
✓ To protect your wind spinner from fading, spray it with a UV-resistant clear spray. Allow it to dry before hanging.

CHAPTER 8
ACRYLIC & PLASTIC

NIGHT LIGHT PLATE ACRYLIC

ALSO: Flat ornaments

This recipe is for an acrylic nightlight plate for a light-up base, these come in a variety of shapes.

INGREDIENTS
☐ Acrylic nightlight blank
☐ Blowout paper (two sheets)
☐ Heat-resistant tape
☐ Sublimation transfer (print/sheet)

EQUIPMENT
☐ Microfiber cloth
☐ Rubbing alcohol
☐ Flat heat source such as a heat press

PREPARATION

Start with a new acrylic blank for the best results.

Pre-heat your flat heat press to the temperature shown in the chart below.

Remove any plastic protective film from the acrylic. **Gently clean it with rubbing alcohol and a microfiber cloth** to remove any debris or residue.

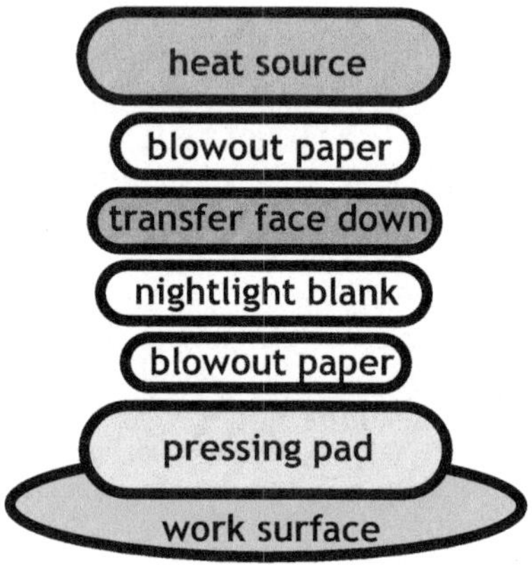

Trim the edges of your printed sublimation transfer, maintaining a size slightly larger than your acrylic blank.

Place your sublimation transfer sheet face up on your work surface. **Lay your acrylic nightlight blank face down** on top. **Secure it in place** on all sides using heat-resistant tape.

Place a sheet of blowout paper (I recommend white cardstock or butcher paper) on top of your pressing pad.

Position your acrylic blank with sublimation transfer side up on top of the blowout paper.

Place another sheet of blowout paper on top.

Press as indicated in the chart below.

After pressing, use heat-resistant gloves to remove the acrylic blank from the heated surface immediately.

Place the acrylic blank between two heavy objects to protect from warping that may occur during the cooling process.

When cool, peel the transfer sheet away. If any paper sticks to the blank, soak it in water to help the rest of the paper come off.

heat source
blowout paper
transfer face down
nightlight blank
blowout paper
pressing pad
work surface

COOK TIMES

Here are typical times you can use as a starting point. Always check the manufacturer's instructions for time and temperature, when available.

your favorite settings

Traditional Heat Press	AutoPress	EasyPress	Mini Press	
360°F / 182°C	360°F / 182°C	360°F / 182°C	Medium	
60 seconds	60 seconds	60 seconds	70 seconds	
40 psi (medium pressure)	Auto pressure	Light pressure	Light pressure	

TIPS & TRICKS
✓ If your sublimation transfer sheet sticks to the sublimation blank, simply soak it in water to help remove the paper.

CURVED PHOTO PANEL
ACRYLIC

This recipe uses a sublimation-ready flat acrylic photo panel. You will create the curve!

....

INGREDIENTS
☐ Curved acrylic photo panel
☐ Blowout paper (two sheets)
☐ Heat-resistant tape
☐ Sublimation transfer (print/sheet)

EQUIPMENT
☐ Lint roller
☐ Canister for creative curve
☐ Flat heat source such as a heat press

....

PREPARATION

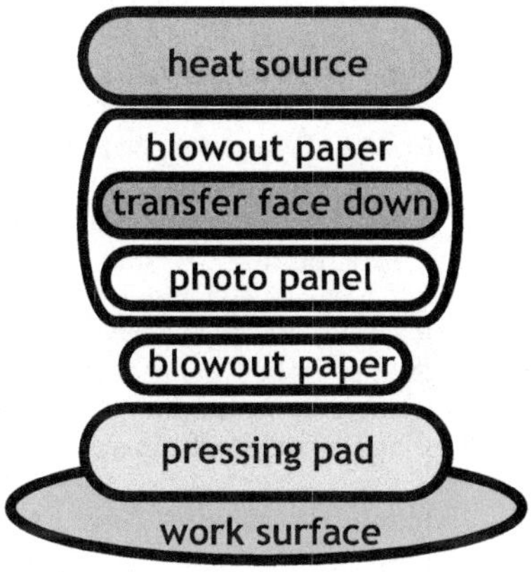

Start with a new acrylic sublimation ready blank for the best results.

Pre-heat your flat heat press to the temperature shown in the chart below.

Trim the edges of your printed sublimation transfer, maintaining a size slightly larger than your acrylic blank.

Remove the protective film from the blank. Take care not to handle to frosted side, which is the sublimation coating, too much.

Cut a **sheet of blowout paper** (I recommend butcher paper) large enough to fold in half and still cover the entire photo panel. Fold the blowout paper in half to crease it.

Open the blowout paper up and **place the sublimation transfer sheet face up** on one half of the blowout paper. **Place the photo panel with the sublimation-ready side down** onto the sublimation transfer sheet.

Carefully turn both the sublimation transfer sheet and panel over. Using **heat-resistant tape**, tape the edges of the sublimation transfer to the blowout paper. Don't let tape overlap with the photo panel.

Fold the other half of the blowout paper over the sublimation transfer sheet and photo panel.

Place a clean sheet of blowout paper (I recommend white cardstock) on top of your pressing pad. Carefully place the folded blowout paper/transfer/panel package on top.

Press according to the chart below. While the panel is pressing, lay the canister on its side. Place a lint roller next to it so the canister stays steady.

When the panel is finished pressing, use heat-resistant gloves to pick up the blowout paper by the sides and gently put it on the canister. Very gently start to slowly pull the sides of the paper downward. Don't pull too hard or too fast. Pull until the panel is curved enough to stand on it's own.

Let the panel cool, then remove the tape and paper.

heat source
blowout paper
transfer face down
photo panel
blowout paper
pressing pad
work surface

....

COOK TIMES

Here are typical times you can use as a starting point. Always check the manufacturer's instructions for time and temperature, when available.

your favorite settings

Traditional Heat Press	AutoPress	EasyPress	Mini Press	
400°F / 204°C	400°F / 204°C	400°F / 204°C	High	
230 seconds	230 seconds	230 seconds	240 seconds	
50 psi (heavy pressure)	Auto pressure	Heavy pressure	Heavy pressure	

....

TIPS & TRICKS
✓ It is strongly recommended to use an autopress or traditional heat press rather than an easypress or mini press.

DOG TAGS ACRYLIC

ALSO: Luggage tags and keychains

This recipe is for single-sided acrylic sublimation dog tags. Different types of acrylic can be more sensitive to heat, so ensure that your product is for sublimation.

INGREDIENTS
☐ Acrylic sublimation blank
☐ Blowout paper (two sheets)
☐ Heat-resistant tape
☐ Sublimation transfer (print/sheet)

EQUIPMENT
☐ Flat heat source such as a heat press
☐ (Optional) Microfiber cloth

PREPARATION

Start with an acrylic sublimation blank.

Pre-heat your flat heat press to the temperature shown in the chart below.

Print a non-mirrored image on your sublimation transfer sheet, and ensure that the image is slightly larger than the acrylic blank.

Remove the protective film from both sides of the acrylic blank. If the film had been removed previously, wipe any dust or debris away using a microfiber cloth.

Place a piece of blowout paper on top of your pressing pad.

Place the **transfer sheet on top of the blowout paper** with the image facing up.

Align the acrylic blank with the sublimation side down on top of the transfer sheet.

Using the **heat-resistant tape, secure the acrylic blank to the transfer sheet.**

Cover with the second piece of blowout paper and press according to the chart below.

Remove immediately from the press and place under something heavy while the item cools. This will prevent the acrylic from warping during the cooling process.

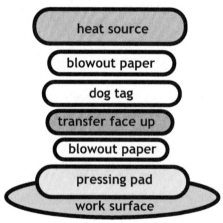

heat source
blowout paper
dog tag
transfer face up
blowout paper
pressing pad
work surface

COOK TIMES
Here are typical times you can use as a starting point. Always check the manufacturer's instructions for time and temperature, when available.

your favorite settings

Traditional Heat Press	AutoPress	EasyPress	Mini Press	
400°F / 204°C	400°F / 204°C	385°F / 196°C	High	
60 seconds	45 seconds	40 seconds	70 seconds	
40 psi (medium pressure)	Auto pressure	Light pressure	Light pressure	

TIPS & TRICKS
✗ To help avoid the sublimation transfer from sticking to the acrylic remove while warm.
✓ You can add heat-transfer vinyl to the back of the acrylic blank to help the sublimated image stand out.
✓ If your sublimation transfer sheet sticks to the sublimation blank, simply soak it in water to help remove the paper.
✓ After Care: Wash sublimated acrylic in warm soapy water to remove dirt and debris.

KEYCHAINS ACRYLIC

ALSO: Luggage tags

This recipe is for single-sided acrylic sublimation keychains. Different types of acrylic can be more sensitive to heat, so ensure that your product is for sublimation.

INGREDIENTS
☐ Acrylic sublimation blank
☐ Blowout paper (two sheets)
☐ Heat-resistant tape
☐ Sublimation transfer (print/sheet)

EQUIPMENT
☐ Flat heat source such as a heat press
☐ (Optional) Microfiber cloth
☐ (Optional) Heavy book or item to place on top of keychain

PREPARATION

Start with an acrylic sublimation blank.

Pre-heat your flat heat press to the temperature shown in the chart below.

Very closely trim your sublimation transfer design, ensuring that the image is slightly larger than the acrylic blank.

Remove the protective film from both sides of the acrylic blank. If the film had been removed previously, wipe any dust or debris away using a microfiber cloth.

Place a piece of blowout paper on top of your pressing pad.

Place the sublimation print face up on the table. Place the acrylic blank face down on top of the print. **Secure with heat-resistant tape.**

Place a clean sheet of blowout paper on your pressing pad.

Place the acrylic blank on top of the blowout paper with the sublimation transfer as the top layer.

Cover with the second piece of blowout paper and press according to the chart below.

Remove immediately from the press and place under something heavy while the item cools. This will prevent the acrylic from warping during the cooling process.

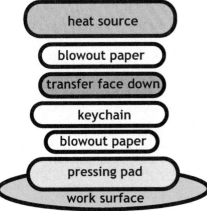

heat source
blowout paper
transfer face down
keychain
blowout paper
pressing pad
work surface

COOK TIMES
Here are typical times you can use as a starting point. Always check the manufacturer's instructions for time and temperature, when available.

your favorite settings

Traditional Heat Press	AutoPress	EasyPress	Mini Press	
370°F / 188°C	370°F / 188°C	370°F / 188°C	High	
60 seconds	45 seconds	60 seconds	60 seconds	
40 psi (medium pressure)	Auto pressure	Light pressure	Light pressure	

TIPS & TRICKS
✗ To help avoid the sublimation transfer from sticking to the acrylic, remove while warm.
✓ You can add heat-transfer vinyl to the back of the acrylic blank to help the sublimated image stand out.
✓ If your sublimation transfer sheet sticks to the sublimation blank, simply soak it in water to help remove the paper.
✓ After Care: Wash sublimated acrylic in warm soapy water to remove dirt and debris.

BUSINESS CARDS ACRYLIC

ALSO: ID cards and gift cards

This recipe is for a two sided acrylic sublimation business card blank.

INGREDIENTS
☐ Business card sublimation blanc
☐ Blowout paper (two sheets)
☐ Heat-resistant tape
☐ Sublimation transfer(s) (print/sheet)

EQUIPMENT
☐ Microfiber cloth
☐ Flat heat source such as a heat press

PREPARATION

Start with an acrylic sublimation blank.

Pre-heat your flat heat press to the temperature shown in the chart below.

Trim the edges of your printed sublimation transfer to align with the size and shape of your sublimation blank. Ensure that your print is trimmed slightly larger than the blank.

Peel off the clear protective layer off of the acrylic blank. If there is a white sublimation layer, leave it intact. If you previously removed the protective layer, wipe off the blank with a microfiber cloth to remove any dust or debris before sublimating.

Place a **piece of blowout paper (I recommend white cardstock or butcher paper)** onto your pressing pad.

Place your **sublimation print with the print side up** on the blowout paper.

Align and place your acrylic blank with the white side down on top of the transfer paper. **Secure with heat-resistant tape.**

If you are **sublimating both sides of the business card,** you will place the second transfer sheet face down on top of the back side of the acrylic blank. If you wish to sublimate one side at a time, it is recommended to allow the blank to cool for at least 60 seconds in between sublimations.

Place your second piece of blowout paper directly on top of the acrylic blank.

Press according to the chart below.

Using heat-resistant gloves, remove the acrylic blank from the work surface. **Peel away the transfer sheet(s)** while the item is still warm.

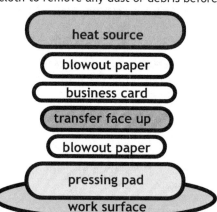

heat source
blowout paper
business card
transfer face up
blowout paper
pressing pad
work surface

COOK TIMES
Here are typical times you can use as a starting point. Always check the manufacturer's instructions for time and temperature, when available.

your favorite settings

Traditional Heat Press	AutoPress	EasyPress	Mini Press	
400°F / 204°C	400°F / 204°C	385°F / 196°C	High	
60 seconds	45 seconds	40 seconds	70 seconds	
40 psi (medium pressure)	Auto pressure	Light pressure	Light pressure	

TIPS & TRICKS
✓ Some acrylic blanks will warp during cooling. Remove quickly from the heated workspace and place under a book to cool. You can also use a heat press that is cooled.

ORNAMENTS ACRYLIC

ALSO: Gift tags

This recipe is for a sublimation-ready acrylic blank. One side of the blank will have a white coating, and the other side will have a protective layer.

INGREDIENTS
☐ Sublimation ready acrylic blank
☐ Blowout paper (two sheets)
☐ Heat-resistant tape
☐ Sublimation transfer (print/sheet)

EQUIPMENT
☐ Flat heat source such as a heat press
☐ (Optional) Microfiber cloth

PREPARATION

Start with an acrylic sublimation blank.

Pre-heat your flat heat press to the temperature shown in the chart below.

Trim the edges of your printed sublimation transfer to align with the size and shape of your sublimation blank. Ensure that your print is trimmed slightly larger than the blank.

Peel off the clear protective layer off the acrylic blank, leaving the white sublimation layer intact. If you previously removed the protective layer, simply wipe off the blank with a microfiber cloth to remove any dust or debris prior to sublimating.

Place a **piece of blowout paper** (I recommend white cardstock or butcher paper) onto your pressing pad.

Place your **sublimation print with the print side up** on the blowout paper.

Align and place your acrylic blank with the white side down on top of the transfer paper. Secure with heat-resistant tape.

Place your second piece of blowout paper directly on top of the acrylic blank.

Press according to the chart below.

Using heat-resistant gloves, remove the acrylic blank from the work surface. **Next, peel away the transfer** while the item is still warm.

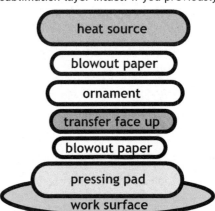

COOK TIMES
Here are typical times you can use as a starting point. Always check the manufacturer's instructions for time and temperature, when available.

your favorite settings

Traditional Heat Press	AutoPress	EasyPress	Mini Press	
400°F / 204°C	400°F / 204°C	385°F / 196°C	High	
60 seconds	45 seconds	40 seconds	70 seconds	
40 psi (medium pressure)	Auto pressure	Light pressure	Light pressure	

TIPS & TRICKS
✗ To avoid the paper sticking to the acrylic remove the transfer sheet while the blank is still warm.
✓ For a tutorial check out jennifermaker.com/diy-sublimation-ornaments/
✓ Placing the acrylic on top of the transfer sheet allows the acrylic to absorb the most heat.

PLACE CARD SIGNS ACRYLIC

ALSO: Acrylic cake toppers and acrylic award plaques

This recipe is for a sublimation-ready acrylic place card sign.

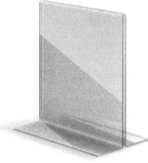

INGREDIENTS
☐ Acrylic sublimation blank place card sign
☐ Blowout paper (two sheets)
☐ Heat-resistant tape
☐ Sublimation transfer (print/sheet)

EQUIPMENT
☐ Lint roller or microfiber cloth
☐ Flat heat source such as a heat press

PREPARATION

Start with a new acrylic sublimation ready blank for the best results.

Pre-heat your flat heat press to the temperature shown in the chart below.

Remove any plastic protective film from the sublimation blank.

Trim the edges of your printed sublimation transfer, maintaining a size slightly larger than your acrylic blank. For blanks with a base or edge, you will trim to the very edge of the sublimation surface.

If your item has a base, you will need to **create a working surface** that will allow the bottom of the blank to sit over the edge of the heating space. This may include additional pressing pads or a pillow to provide the necessary height.

Place a piece of blowout paper (I recommend white cardstock or butcher paper) on top of your pressing pad, and the additional pillow or foam.

Place your transfer sheet face-side up on top of the blowout paper.

Position your sublimation blank with the sublimation side down on top of the transfer paper.

Use **heat-resistant tape** to secure the blank to the transfer paper to help prevent ghosting and the transfer from slipping during pressing.

Place the **second piece of blowout paper** on top of your sublimation blank.

Press as indicated in the chart below.

After pressing, **use heat-resistant gloves to remove the acrylic blank** from the heated surface immediately. **Peel away the tranfer print while still warm.**

Place the acrylic blank between two heavy objects to protect from warping that may occur during the cooling process.

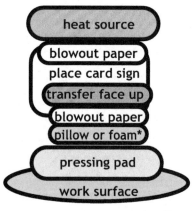

* optional

COOK TIMES

Here are typical times you can use as a starting point. Always check the manufacturer's instructions for time and temperature, when available.

your favorite settings

Traditional Heat Press	AutoPress	EasyPress	Mini Press	
400°F / 204°C	400°F / 204°C	385°F / 196°C	High	
60 seconds	45 seconds	40 seconds	70 seconds	
40 psi (medium pressure)	Auto pressure	Light pressure	Light pressure	

TIPS & TRICKS
✗ Acrylic will get hot during the sublimation process. Wear your heat-resistant gloves to protect yourself.
✓ After Care: Rubbing alcohol can be used to clean heavy grime off of sublimated items.

FAUX LEATHER POLYURETHANE
ALSO: Journals, planners, sheets

This recipe is for sublimation-ready faux leather blanks. If you have a non-sublimation faux leather blank, you will need to perform additional steps to prepare for this sublimation recipe.

INGREDIENTS
☐ Faux leather sublimation blank
☐ Blowout paper (two sheets)
☐ Heat-resistant tape
☐ Mirrored sublimation transfer (print/sheet)

EQUIPMENT
☐ Lint roller
☐ Flat heat source such as a heat press
☐ (Optional) Ruler for placement help

PREPARATION

Start with your faux leather sublimation blank. If you are not using a pre-cut blank, you will want to cut the faux leather into the desired shape.

Pre-heat your flat heat press to the temperature shown in the chart below.

Trim the edges of your printed sublimation transfer to minimize the appearance of paper lines on your finished product. If you are able, you will want the print to be larger than your sublimation blank.

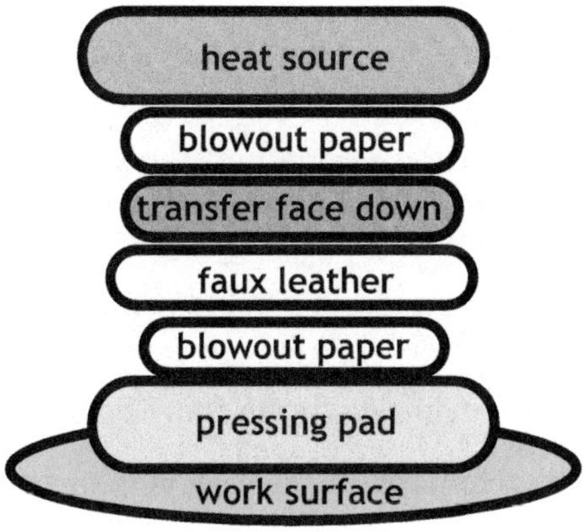

Place a piece of blowout paper on top of your pressing pad.

Set your faux leather blank with the top facing up on top of your blowout paper.

Align and tape all four edges of your design face down on your faux leather blank. To prevent ghosting, you will want to ensure that the print extends beyond the edge of the faux leather.

Place the second piece of blowout paper on top of the sublimation transfer.

Press according to the chart below.

Using heat-resistant gloves, remove from press and peel transfer away from faux leather while still warm.

heat source
blowout paper
transfer face down
faux leather
blowout paper
pressing pad
work surface

COOK TIMES
Here are typical times you can use as a starting point. Always check the manufacturer's instructions for time and temperature, when available.

your favorite settings

Traditional Heat Press	AutoPress	EasyPress	Mini Press	
350°F / 180°C	380°F / 196°C	380°F / 196°C	High	
60 seconds	45 seconds	40 seconds	70 seconds	
40 psi (medium pressure)	Auto pressure	Light pressure	Light pressure	

TIPS & TRICKS
× Don't remove your sublimation transfer sheet for at least 10 seconds so it can cool down without ghosting.
✓ If sublimating a faux leather journal, you want the cover flat for pressing. You will need to remove the inside pages to lay the cover flat.
✓ When choosing faux leather for sublimation, look for one that has a smooth surface rather than a pebbled texture.

WATCHBAND POLYLEATHER/PLASTIC

Personalized watchbands can be a great DIY gift or way to accessorize your own watch.

INGREDIENTS
☐ Sublimation watchband blank
☐ Blowout paper (two sheets)
☐ Heat-resistant tape
☐ Sublimation transfer (print/sheet)

EQUIPMENT
☐ Lint roller
☐ Flat heat source such as a heat press
☐ (Optional) Heat resistant gloves

PREPARATION

Prepare the watchband for sublimation by removing the loop from the watchband, and remove any protective plastic.

Pre-heat your flat heat press to the temperature shown in the chart below.

Lay blowout paper on your work surface. Place the watchband with the sublimation side facing up on top of the blowout paper.

Using the lint roller, remove any dust or debris from the watch band.

Secure the sublimation transfer to the watch band using heat-resistant tape. You want to ensure that the image extends just beyond the edges of the watch band.

Place the second piece of blowout paper on top of the sublimation transfer.

Press according to the chart below.

Allow to cool before removing the sublimation transfer sheet.

Re-assemble the watch band.

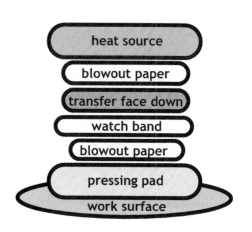

heat source
blowout paper
transfer face down
watch band
blowout paper
pressing pad
work surface

COOK TIMES
Here are typical times you can use as a starting point. Always check the manufacturer's instructions for time and temperature, when available.

your favorite settings

Traditional Heat Press	AutoPress	EasyPress	Mini Press	
375°F / 191°C	375°F / 191°C	375°F / 191°C	Medium	
50 seconds	50 seconds	50 seconds	40 seconds	
30 psi (Light pressure)	Light pressure	Light pressure	Light pressure	

TIPS & TRICKS
✓ Remember to mirror your design if it includes words.
✓ To clean the watch band you can use a mild dish soap and water.
✗ Don't remove your sublimation transfer sheet for at least 10 seconds so it can cool down without ghosting.

ID BADGES PVC

ALSO: Luggage tags, plastic cards, and badge reels

This recipe is for PVC Plastic sublimation approved flat blanks.

INGREDIENTS
☐ Sublimation approved PVC blank
☐ Blowout paper (two sheets)
☐ Heat-resistant tape
☐ Sublimation transfer(s) (print/sheet)

EQUIPMENT
☐ Lint roller
☐ Flat heat source such as a heat press

PREPARATION

Start with a PVC Sublimation blank.

Pre-heat your flat heat press to the temperature shown in the chart below.

Trim the edges of your printed sublimation transfer to minimize the appearance of paper lines on your finished product. If you are able, you will want the print to be larger than your sublimation blank. If you are sublimating on both sides, prepare both transfer sheets.

Remove any plastic protective film from your sublimation blank. If there is no protective film, use a lint roller to remove any dust or debris.

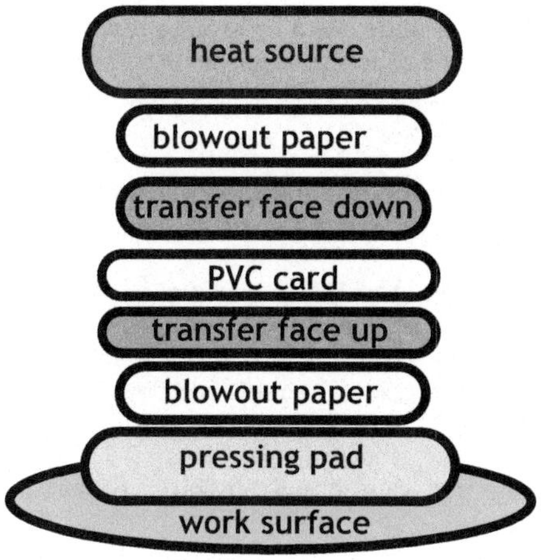

Place a piece of blowout paper on the pressing pad.

Place the **bottom transfer sheet face-side up** on top of the blowout paper.

Align your sublimation blank on top of the bottom transfer sheet and then place the top transfer sheet face-side down on top of the sublimation blank.

Secure with heat-resistant tape to avoid ghosting or the images moving during pressing.

Place a piece of blowout paper on top of the transfer sheet.

Press according to the times listed in the chart below.

Using **heat-resistant gloves, remove from the work surface** and pull the transfer sheet while warm.

heat source
blowout paper
transfer face down
PVC card
transfer face up
blowout paper
pressing pad
work surface

COOK TIMES
Here are typical times you can use as a starting point. Always check the manufacturer's instructions for time and temperature, when available.

your favorite settings

Traditional Heat Press	AutoPress	EasyPress	Mini Press	
400°F / 204°C	400°F / 204°C	365°F / 185°C	High	
60 seconds	60 seconds	55 seconds	70 seconds	
40 psi (medium pressure)	Auto pressure	Medium pressure	Light pressure	

TIPS & TRICKS
✗ For plastic items remove your transfer sheet quickly after sublimating using heat-resistant gloves.
✓ To avoid warping, use a heavy book to place on top of the PVC cards after sublimating.
✓ After Care: Use a microfiber cloth to remove dirt or debris. You can use rubbing alcohol for heavier grime.

FRISBEES PVC PLASTIC
ALSO: Frisbee rings and fans

This recipe is for a PVC plastic sublimation frisbee blank.

INGREDIENTS
☐ Frisbee blank - PVC plastic
☐ Blowout paper (two sheets)
☐ Heat-resistant tape
☐ Mirrored sublimation transfer (print/sheet)

EQUIPMENT
☐ Microfiber cloth
☐ Flat heat source such as a heat press
☐ Foam or towel to fill the inside of blank

PREPARATION

Start with a sublimation-approved PVC blank frisbee.

Pre-heat your flat heat press to the temperature shown in the chart below.

Remove any plastic protective film from the sublimation blank.

Trim the edges of your printed sublimation transfer to minimize the appearance of paper lines on your finished product. If you are able, you will want the print to be larger than your sublimation blank.

If your frisbee has a lip around the edge, create a foam insert to ensure that you can press the sublimation transfer to the top of the frisbee without warping the shape of the disc. Alternatively, you can use a towel rolled into the body of the disc.

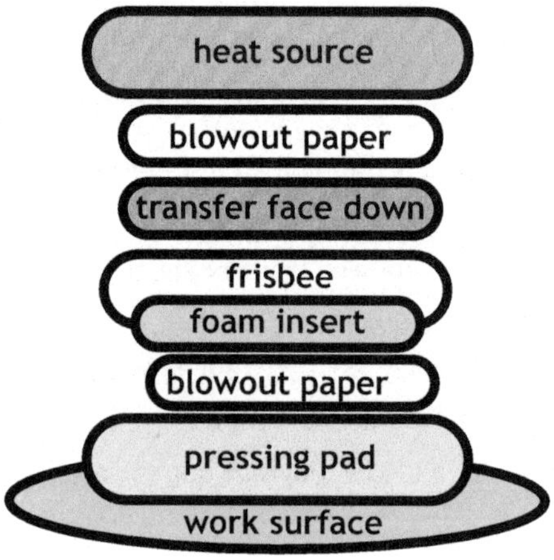

Place a **piece of blowout paper (I recommend white cardstock or butcher paper)** on top of your pressing pad.

Place the foam insert or towel and the frisbee with the sublimation side facing up on top of the blowout paper.

Place the transfer sheet face down on top of the sublimation side of the frisbee.

Tape the edges of your design face down onto your frisbee using heat-resistant tape.

Place a piece of blowout paper on top of the transfer sheet.

Press according to the times listed in the chart below.

Using **heat-resistant gloves, remove from the work surface** and pull the transfer sheet while warm.

heat source
blowout paper
transfer face down
frisbee
foam insert
blowout paper
pressing pad
work surface

COOK TIMES
Here are typical times you can use as a starting point. Always check the manufacturer's instructions for time and temperature, when available.

your favorite settings

Traditional Heat Press	AutoPress	EasyPress	Mini Press	
355°F / 179°C	355°F / 179°C	365°F / 185°C	High	
90 seconds	60 seconds	55 seconds	70 seconds	
40 psi (medium pressure)	Auto pressure	Medium pressure	Light pressure	

TIPS & TRICKS
✗ Do not use a higher temp for plastic blanks. This can lead to increased melting or deformation of your product.

MAGNETS FRP

ALSO: Name badge, door plates, and blank sheets

This recipe is for single-sided FRP (fiber-reinfoced plastic) sublimation-ready blanks.

INGREDIENTS
☐ Single sided sublimation blank
☐ Blowout paper (two sheets)
☐ Heat-resistant tape
☐ Mirrored Sublimation transfer (print/sheet)

EQUIPMENT
☐ Microfiber cloth
☐ Flat heat source such as a heat press

PREPARATION

Start with a sublimation-approved FRP sublimation blank.

Pre-heat your flat heat press to the temperature shown in the chart below.

Remove any plastic protective film from both sides of the sublimation blank.

Trim the edges of your printed sublimation transfer so that it just exceeds the blank size.

Do not pre-press the blank, instead hover the blank over the heat press for 10 seconds to remove nay mositure and to heat up the blank.

Place a **piece of blowout paper (I recommend white cardstock or butcher paper)** on top of your pressing pad.

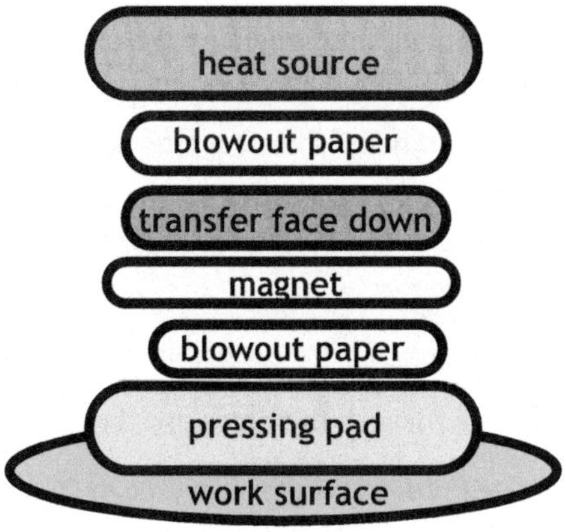

Place your sublimation blank on top of the blowout paper, with the sublimation side facing up.

Place the transfer sheet face down on top of the sublimation side of the blank.

Tape the edges of your design face down onto your blank using heat-resistant tape.

Place a piece of blowout paper on top of the transfer sheet.

Press according to the times listed in the chart below.

Using **heat-resistant gloves, remove from the work surface** and pull the transfer sheet while warm.

| heat source |
| blowout paper |
| transfer face down |
| magnet |
| blowout paper |
| pressing pad |
| work surface |

COOK TIMES
Here are typical times you can use as a starting point. Always check the manufacturer's instructions for time and temperature, when available.

Traditional Heat Press	AutoPress	EasyPress	Mini Press	*your favorite settings*
375°F / 190°C	375°F / 190°C	385°F / 196°C	High	
60 seconds	60 seconds	60 seconds	70 seconds	
40 psi (medium pressure)	Auto pressure	Medium pressure	Light pressure	

TIPS & TRICKS
✗ Do not use a higher temp for plastic blanks. This can lead to increased melting or deformation of your product.
✓ Always use blowout paper and heat-resistant gloves to protect yourself and your press.

DOOR HANGERS FRP

ALSO: Hanging ornament, travel bag tag, and keyring

This recipe is for FRP (fiber-reinfoced plastic) sublimation blanks that are two-sided.

INGREDIENTS
☐ Two sided FRP sublimation blank
☐ Blowout paper (two sheets)
☐ Heat-resistant tape
☐ Sublimation transfer (print/sheet)

EQUIPMENT
☐ Microfiber cloth
☐ Flat heat source such as a heat press

PREPARATION

Start with a sublimation-approved FRP 2-sided sublimation blank.

Pre-heat your flat heat press to the temperature shown in the chart below.

Remove any plastic protective film from both sides of the sublimation blank.

Trim the edges of your printed sublimation transfer so that it just exceeds the blank size.

Hover the blank over the heated press for 10 seconds to remove any moisture and to heat up the blank.

Place a **piece of blowout paper** (I recommend white cardstock or butcher paper) on top of your pressing pad.

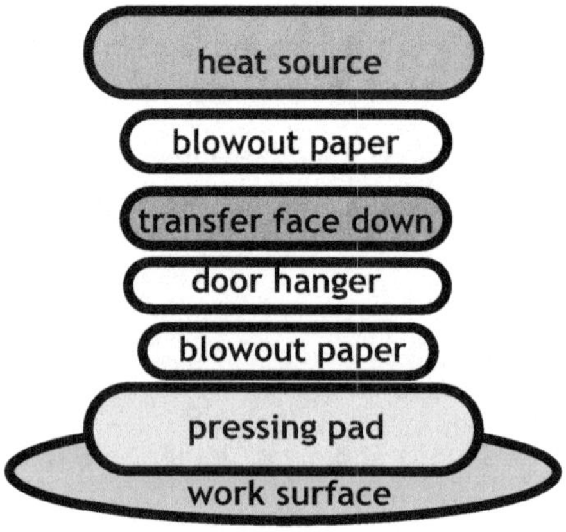

Place your sublimation blank on top of the blowout paper, with either sublimation side facing up.

Place the transfer sheet face down on top of the sublimation side of the blank.

Tape the edges of your design face down onto your blank using heat-resistant tape.

Place a piece of blowout paper on top of the transfer sheet.

Press according to the times listed in the chart below.

Using **heat-resistant gloves, remove from the work surface** and pull the transfer sheet while warm.

Allow the blank to cool entirely before repeating these steps for the other side of the sublimation blank.

| heat source |
| blowout paper |
| transfer face down |
| door hanger |
| blowout paper |
| pressing pad |
| work surface |

COOK TIMES
Here are typical times you can use as a starting point. Always check the manufacturer's instructions for time and temperature, when available.

your favorite settings

Traditional Heat Press	AutoPress	EasyPress	Mini Press	
400°F / 204°C	400°F / 204°C	385°F / 196°C	High	
75-90 seconds	75-90 seconds	60 seconds	70 seconds	
40 psi (medium pressure)	Auto pressure	Medium pressure	Light pressure	

TIPS & TRICKS
✗ Do not attempt to sublimate both sides at the same time. You can not imprint both sides at the same time.
✓ Always use blowout paper and heat-resistant gloves to protect yourself and your press.

CHAPTER 9
WOOD

PLAQUES WOOD

ALSO: Trophy plaque

These come in various shapes, including squares, circles, sports-related, etc.; however, they must have a sublimation surface.

INGREDIENTS
☐ Plaque sublimation blank
☐ Blowout paper (two sheets)
☐ Heat-resistant tape
☐ Sublimation transfer (print/sheet)

EQUIPMENT
☐ Lint roller
☐ Flat heat source such as a heat press

PREPARATION

Start with a wood plaque sublimation blank. This will have a white sublimation surface on one side.

Remove the protective cover from the plaque. If you have previously removed the protective cover, then you should use a lint roller to remove any dust or debris from the sublimation surface.

Pre-heat your flat heat press to the temperature shown in the chart below.

Very closely trim the edges of your printed sublimation transfer to ensure that the transfer is slightly larger than your sublimation surface.

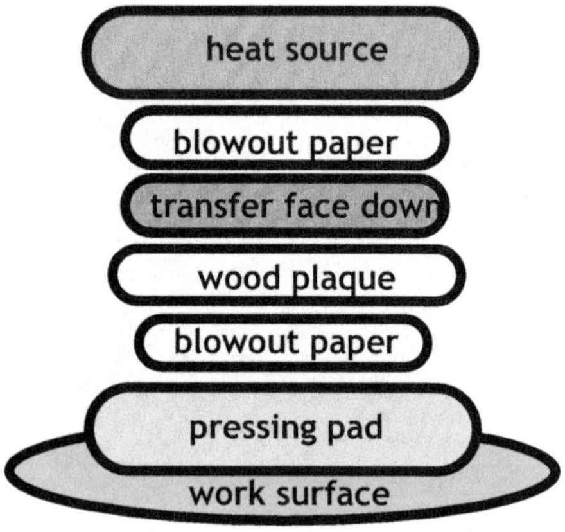

Place a piece of blowout paper (I recommend white cardstock or butcher paper) on the pressing pad.

Place the transfer sheet on top of the sublimation blank. Ensure that the mounting slots on the back of the blank are in the correct position.

Crease your sublimation transfer along the edge of the plaque, and fold the edge of the transfer over the back side of the plaque. **Using heat-resistant tape,** secure the transfer to the back side of the blank on the top and the bottom sides of the plaque.

Place the sublimation blank on top of the blowout paper with the sublimation side facing up and the transfer sheet facing down.

Place a piece of blowout paper on the top of the transfer sheeet.

Press according to the chart below.

Allow to cool before removing the transfer sheet. Use heat-resistant gloves when removing the blank from the pressing surface.

heat source
blowout paper
transfer face down
wood plaque
blowout paper
pressing pad
work surface

* optional

COOK TIMES
Here are typical times you can use as a starting point. Always check the manufacturer's instructions for time and temperature, when available.

your favorite settings

Traditional Heat Press	AutoPress	EasyPress	Mini Press	
400°F / 204°C	400°F / 204°C	385°F / 196°C	High	
60 seconds	60 seconds	60 seconds	70 seconds	
40 psi (medium pressure)	Auto pressure	Light pressure	Light pressure	

TIPS & TRICKS
✓ For a tutorial check out jennifermaker.com/sublimation-on-wood/

GARDEN STAKES PLYWOOD

ALSO: Wood cake toppers and wood label signs

This recipe is for wood garden stake sublimation blanks. These can be sublimated on either side and come in various shapes and sizes.

INGREDIENTS
☐ Garden stake sublimation blank
☐ Blowout paper (two sheets)
☐ Heat-resistant tape
☐ Sublimation transfer(s) (print/sheet)

EQUIPMENT
☐ Lint roller
☐ Flat heat source such as a heat press

PREPARATION

Start with a garden stake sublimation blank. These can be sublimated on both sides.

Pre-heat your flat heat press to the temperature shown in the chart below.

Trim the edges of your printed sublimation transfer so that there is a little extra to go around the edge of the sublimation blank.

Place a piece of blowout paper (I recommend white cardstock or butcher paper) on your pressing pad.

Place the sublimation blank on top of the blowout paper and cover it with a second sheet of blowout paper.

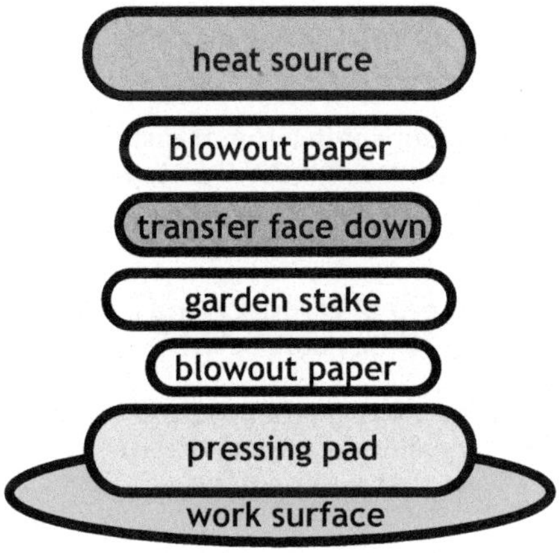

Pre-press your sublimation blank for 10 seconds to remove any excess moisture. **Allow to cool for a few seconds** before removing the top sheet of blowout paper.

Place the sublimation transfer sheet face down on top of the sublimation blank.

Using heat-resistant tape, secure the transfer sheet to the blank, allowing the edge of the design to extend beyond the edge of the blank.

Place a piece of blowout paper on top of the transfer sheet.

Press as indicated in the chart below.

Allow to cool before removing the transfer sheet.

Repeat the process if you wish to sublimate the other side. You will not need to pre-press the blank to eliminate mositure for the second sublimation.

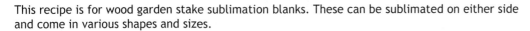

heat source

blowout paper

transfer face down

garden stake

blowout paper

pressing pad

work surface

COOK TIMES
Here are typical times you can use as a starting point. Always check the manufacturer's instructions for time and temperature, when available.

your favorite settings

Traditional Heat Press	AutoPress	EasyPress	Mini Press	
375°F / 190°C	375°F / 190°C	380°F / 194°C	High	
50 seconds	50 seconds	45 seconds	70 seconds	
40 psi (medium pressure)	Auto pressure	Light pressure	Light pressure	

TIPS & TRICKS
✓ For a tutorial check out jennifermaker.com/sublimation-on-wood/

SIGNS WOOD

These signs often come in many shapes and sizes. These blanks will usually have a white sublimation surface.

INGREDIENTS
☐ Sublimation wood blank
☐ Blowout paper (two sheets)
☐ Piece of cardstock
☐ Heat-resistant tape
☐ Sublimation transfer

EQUIPMENT
☐ Lint roller
☐ Flat heat source such as a heat press
☐ (Optional) Picture hanger

PREPARATION

Start with a sublimation wood blank.

Pre-heat your flat heat press to the temperature shown in the chart below.

Remove the protective plastic from both sides of the sublimation blank.

Pre-pressing your wood blank is very important to remove any moisture from the wood. First, place a clean piece of blowout paper (I recommend white cardstock or butcher paper) on your pressing pad, followed by your wood blank with the sublimation side facing up, then another piece of blowout paper. Press for 50 seconds.

Prepare your sublimation transfer sheet. You do not need to trim the edges; simply place the full sheet on top of the sublimation blank face down.

Using heat-resistant tape, secure your sublimation blank in place.

Place a piece of cardstock and blowout paper on top, then press as indicated in the chart below.

When done, you can **remove the cardstock and blowout paper**; however, allow to **cool before removing the heat-resistant tape and transfer sheet.**

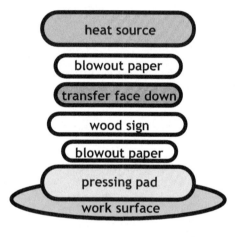

heat source

blowout paper

transfer face down

wood sign

blowout paper

pressing pad

work surface

COOK TIMES
Here are typical times you can use as a starting point. Always check the manufacturer's instructions for time and temperature, when available.

your favorite settings

Traditional Heat Press	AutoPress	EasyPress	Mini Press	
385°F / 196°C	385°F / 204°C	385°F / 196°C	High	
90 seconds	90 seconds	60 seconds	70 seconds	
40 psi (medium pressure)	Auto pressure	Light pressure	Light pressure	

TIPS & TRICKS
✕ Wood can get very hot in the press so make sure to use heat-resistant gloves when handling.
✓ If your sublimation transfer sheet sticks to the wood, simply use a damp cloth or sponge and remove the paper.
✓ For a tutorial check out jennifermaker.com/sublimation-on-wood/

CHARCUTERIE BOARDS WOOD

ALSO: Wood cutting boards

This recipe is for wood charcuterie board sublimation blanks, which can include wood cutting boards these come in a variety of sizes.

INGREDIENTS
☐ Wood sublimation blank
☐ Blowout paper (two sheets)
☐ Heat-resistant tape
☐ Sublimation transfer (print/sheet)

EQUIPMENT
☐ Lint roller
☐ Flat heat source such as a heat press

PREPARATION

Start with a sublimation ready charcuterie board blank.

Pre-heat your flat heat press to the temperature shown in the chart below.

Use a lint roller to remove any dust or debris from your blank.

Pre-press the wood blank betweem two pieces of blowout paper (I recommend white cardstock or butcher paper) for 60 seconds to remove any moisture.

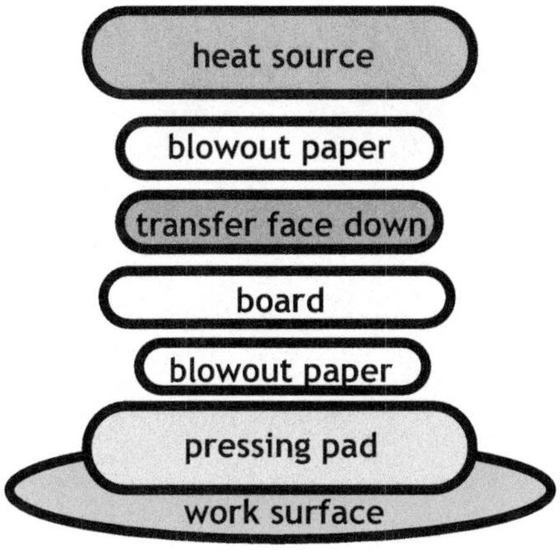

Trim the edges of your transfer sheet so that there is a little bit that goes over the ends of the sublimation space. If you only plan to sublimate a portion, very closely trim the edges to avoid the appearance of lines on your finished product.

Align and then attach the transfer sheet to the sublimation blank using heat-resistant tape.

Place a **piece of blowout paper** on the pressing pad.

Place the sublimation blank on top of the blowout paper with the transfer sheet attached face down onto the board.

Place a sheet of blowout paper on top of the back side of the transfer sheet.

Press according to the chart below.

Using heat-resistant gloves, remove the board from the pressing surface immediately.

Remove the transfer sheet from the substrate.

heat source

blowout paper

transfer face down

board

blowout paper

pressing pad

work surface

COOK TIMES
Here are typical times you can use as a starting point. Always check the manufacturer's instructions for time and temperature, when available.

your favorite settings

Traditional Heat Press	AutoPress	EasyPress	Mini Press	
385°F / 196°C	385°F / 196°C	385°F / 196°C	High	
120 - 150 seconds	120-150 seconds	100 seconds	90 seconds	
40 psi (medium pressure)	Auto pressure	Light pressure	Light pressure	

TIPS & TRICKS
× Do not sublimate on both sides, you can only sublimate on the lighter side of the board.

CHAPTER 10
VINYL, PAPER, CARDBOARD, & CARDSTOCK

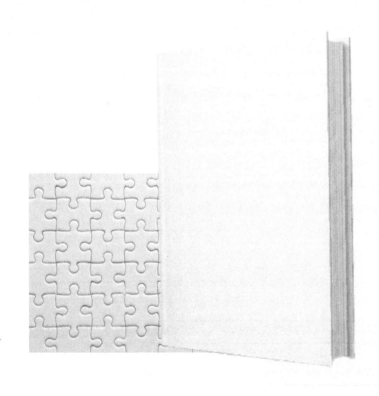

STICKERS SUBLIDECAL PAPER

ALSO: Decals and labels

This recipe is for sublimation stickers using a sublimation sticker sheet. These are waterproof and can be applied to a variety of surfaces.

INGREDIENTS

☐ Sublimation sticker sheet
☐ Blowout paper (two sheets)
☐ Heat-resistant tape
☐ Sublimation transfer (print/sheet)

EQUIPMENT

☐ Lint roller
☐ Flat heat source such as a heat press
☐ Scissors
☐ (Optional) Cutting machine to cut out stickers

PREPARATION

Start with a blank sheet of sticker sublimation paper.

Pre-heat your flat **heat press** to the temperature shown in the chart below.

Do not trim your sublimation transfer sheet.

Place a sheet of blowout paper on the pressing pad.

Place the sublimation sticker sheet face up on the blowout paper.

Align and place your sublimation transfer face down on the sticker sheet.

Using heat-resistant tape, secure the transfer sheet to the sticker sheet on the top and bottom edges. Next, fold the tape onto the back side of the paper.

Place a piece of blowout paper on top of the transfer sheet.

Press according to the chart below.

When finished, **remove the sheets from the press.** Pull the transfer sheet from the sticker sheet as quickly as possible.

Then cut your stickers using either a cutting machine or scissors.

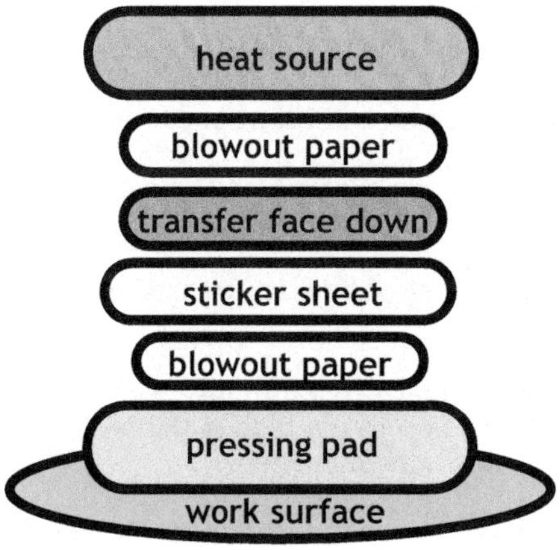

| heat source |
| blowout paper |
| transfer face down |
| sticker sheet |
| blowout paper |
| pressing pad |
| work surface |

COOK TIMES

Here are typical times you can use as a starting point. Always check the manufacturer's instructions for time and temperature, when available.

your favorite settings

Traditional Heat Press	AutoPress	EasyPress	Mini Press	
345°F / 174°C	345°F / 174°C	385°F / 196°C	High	
180-210 seconds	180-210 seconds	40 seconds	70 seconds	
40 psi (medium pressure)	Auto pressure	Mediumpressure	Medium pressure	

TIPS & TRICKS

✓ After 72 hours, the sticker is waterproof and cannot be removed from the surface.
✓ If you are using a cutting machine, you will want to use the print then cut option, using your sublimation printer as the printer and then your machine as the cutting machine. You can also cut out your stickers with scissors when completed.

PUZZLES CARDBOARD

This recipe is for cardboard sublimation blanks. They come in various sizes and shapes, including squares, rectangles, hearts, circles, large and small puzzles, etc.

INGREDIENTS
☐ Sublimation puzzle blank
☐ Blowout paper (two sheets)
☐ Heat-resistant tape
☐ Sublimation transfer (print/sheet)

EQUIPMENT
☐ Microfiber cloth
☐ Flat heat source such as a heat press

PREPARATION

Start with a puzzle sublimation blank.

Pre-heat your flat heat press to the temperature shown in the chart below.

Place your sublimation blank between two pieces of blowout paper and pre-press for 20 seconds. This is important to remove the mositure from the puzzle blank.

After allowing blank to cool, remove any excess moisture with a microfiber cloth.

Place a **piece of blowout paper** on your pressing pad.

Place your puzzle blank with the sublimation side up on the blowout paper.

Align the sublimation transfer sheet face down on top of the sublimation blank.

Using heat-resistant tape, secure the transfer sheet to the sublimation blank. Secure the tape to the back side of the blank to avoid visible tape lines after sublimation.

Place a **piece of blowout paper** on top of the transfer sheet.

Press according to the chart below.

Using heat-resistant gloves, remove from the press.

Remove the sublimation transfer sheet and allow the item to cool.

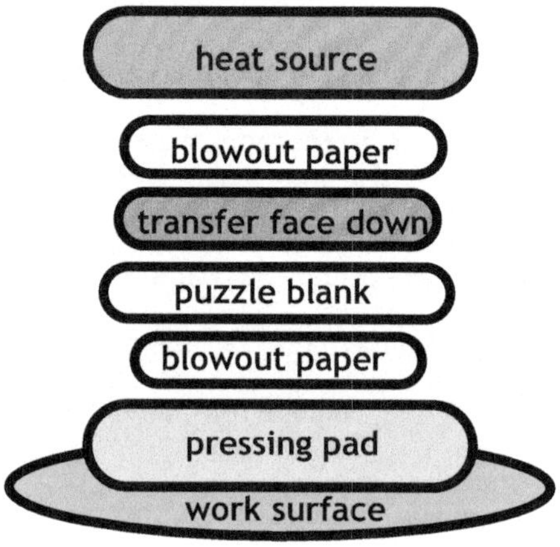

heat source
blowout paper
transfer face down
puzzle blank
blowout paper
pressing pad
work surface

COOK TIMES
Here are typical times you can use as a starting point. Always check the manufacturer's instructions for time and temperature, when available.

your favorite settings

Traditional Heat Press	AutoPress	EasyPress	Mini Press	
385°F / 196°C	400°F / 204°C	385°F / 196°C	High	
45-60 seconds	45 seconds	40 seconds	70 seconds	
40 psi (medium pressure)	Auto pressure	Light pressure	Light pressure	

TIPS & TRICKS
✓ To prevent warping while cooling, place the blank in between two heavy objects during the cooling process.
✓ If your puzzle comes with a backing piece of cardboard, keep it in place while pressing. This will help keep the pieces of the puzzle in place.

NOTEBOOKS CARDBOARD
ALSO: Spiral notebooks

This recipe is for a sublimation notebook cover. These come in both hardbound and spiralbound notebooks.

INGREDIENTS
☐ Sublimation notebook blanks
☐ Blowout paper (two sheets)
☐ Heat-resistant tape
☐ Sublimation transfer (print/sheet)

EQUIPMENT
☐ Lint roller
☐ Flat heat source such as a heat press

PREPARATION

Start with a blank sublimatable cardboard notebook.

Pre-heat your flat heat press to the temperature shown in the chart below.

You must **prepare the notebook to allow the sublimation surface to lay flat.** Remove the spiral and papers from a spiral notebook . Remove the paper and inserts from a cardboard-covered notebook.

Closely trim the edges of your sublimation print to go just to the outside of the sublimation area of the notebook.

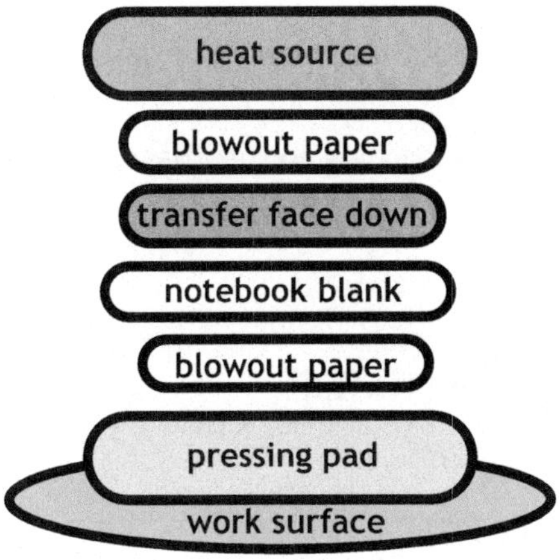

Place a piece of blowout paper (I recommend white cardstock or butcher paper) on the pressing pad.

Remove any protective layer, from the notebook. If there is not a protective layer use a lint roller to remove any dust or debris from the sublimation surface.

Place the sublimation notebook with the sublimation (shiny) side facing up.

Align the sublimation print on top of the sublimation blank. Using heat-resistant tape, secure the transfer sheet to the blank.

Place a piece of blowout paper on top of the transfer sheet.

Press according to the chart below.

Using heat-resistant gloves, remove the sublimation blank from the press.

Carefully remove the sublimation transfer sheet.

Allow item to cool before reassembling the notebook.

heat source
blowout paper
transfer face down
notebook blank
blowout paper
pressing pad
work surface

COOK TIMES
Here are typical times you can use as a starting point. Always check the manufacturer's instructions for time and temperature, when available.

your favorite settings

Traditional Heat Press	AutoPress	EasyPress	Mini Press	
360°F / 182°C	360°F / 182°C	355°F / 179°C	High	
30 seconds	30 seconds	25 seconds	70 seconds	
40 psi (medium pressure)	Auto pressure	Light pressure	Light pressure	

TIPS & TRICKS
✓ If your sublimation comes out light or a little blurry you may need to add a few more seconds or increase pressure.

NAPKIN PAPER

Sublimation on a paper napkin can add a personalized touch to a family get together, holiday event, graduation or wedding party. You can choose to use a cocktail napkin or dinner napkin.

INGREDIENTS
☐ Napkin
☐ Blowout paper (two sheets)
☐ Heat-resistant tape
☐ Sublimation transfer (print/sheet)

EQUIPMENT
☐ Lint roller
☐ Foam roller
☐ Flat heat source such as a heat press

PREPARATION

Start with a new paper napkin for best results. Lightly use a lint roller to clean the surface of your napkin.

Pre-heat your flat heat press to the temperature shown in the chart below.

Lay blowout paper on your work surface. Place the napkin on the blowout paper.

Using heat-resistant tape, secure the sublimation transfer face down on the napkin.

Place another sheet of blowout paper onto the sublimation transfer sheet to prevent ink from bleeding through.

Press according to the chart below. Pull the transfer sheet while still warm.

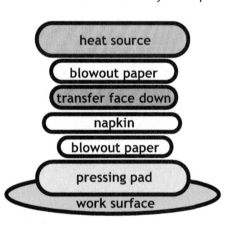

COOK TIMES
Here are typical times you can use as a starting point. Always check the manufacturer's instructions for time and temperature, when available.

your favorite settings

Traditional Heat Press	AutoPress	EasyPress	Mini Press	
400°F / 204°C	400°F / 204°C	400°F / 204°C	High	
60 seconds	60 seconds	60 seconds	60 seconds	
40 psi (Medium pressure)	Auto pressure	Medium pressure	Medium pressure	

TIPS & TRICKS
✓ Remember to mirror your design if it contains words.
✓ Ensure that your sublimation transfer sheet image extends beyond the edge of the napkin.
✓ When using the heat-resistant tape, secure to the blowout paper not the napkin to avoid tearing of the napkin.

GLITTER CARDSTOCK
CARDSTOCK

Sublimation on a white glitter cardstock can help you create beautiful custom cake toppers and other projects.

INGREDIENTS
☐ Sheet of white glitter cardstock
☐ Blowout paper (two sheets)
☐ Heat-resistant tape
☐ Sublimation transfer (print/sheet)

EQUIPMENT
☐ Lint roller
☐ Flat heat source such as a heat press

PREPARATION

Start with a new sheet of white glitter cardstock for best results. Gently use a lint roller to clean the surface of your glitter cardstock.

Pre-heat your flat heat press to the temperature shown in the chart below.

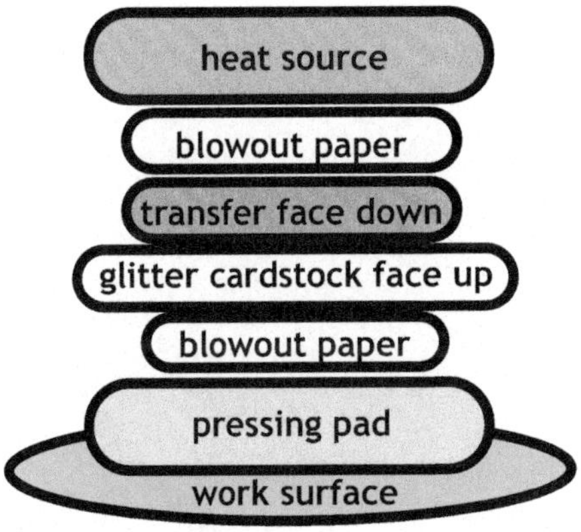

Lay a sheet of blowout paper on your work surface. Place the cardstock glitter side facing up on the blowout paper.

Lay another sheet of blowout paper on top of the cardstock and pre-press for 10 seconds. Remove the top sheet of blowout paper and let the cardstock cool.

Lay the sublimation transfer face down on top of the glitter cardstock.

Using heat-resistant tape, secure the sublimation transfer face down on the glitter cardstock.

Place another sheet of blowout paper onto the sublimation transfer sheet to prevent ink from bleeding through.

Press according to the chart below. Let cool for 10-15 seconds, then pull the transfer sheet while still warm.

heat source
blowout paper
transfer face down
glitter cardstock face up
blowout paper
pressing pad
work surface

COOK TIMES
Here are typical times you can use as a starting point. Always check the manufacturer's instructions for time and temperature, when available.

your favorite settings

Traditional Heat Press	AutoPress	EasyPress	Mini Press	
400°F / 204°C	400°F / 204°C	400°F / 204°C	High	
45 seconds	45 seconds	45 seconds	45 seconds	
40 psi (Medium pressure)	Auto pressure	Medium pressure	Medium pressure	

TIPS & TRICKS
✓ Remember to mirror your design if it contains words.
✓ I recommend using Recollections or Honey Plum brands of glitter cardstock. Dollar Tree brand is not recommended.

CHAPTER 11
NEOPRENE

MOUSEPADS
NEOPRENE AND POLYESTER

This recipe is for a rubber-backed mousepad with a polyester sublimation-approved top. These come in a variety of shapes and can have tan or black rubber backing.

INGREDIENTS
☐ Mousepad sublimation blank
☐ Blowout paper (two sheets)
☐ Heat-resistant tape
☐ Sublimation transfer (print/sheet)

EQUIPMENT
☐ Lint roller
☐ Flat heat source such as a heat press

PREPARATION

Start with a sublimation-ready mousepad.

Pre-heat your flat heat press to the temperature shown in the chart below.

Ensure that your sublimation print extends beyond the edge of the mousepad. Also, ensure that if you have any words on your print, you have mirrored your image correctly.

Place a piece of blowout paper (I recommend white cardstock or butcher paper) on the pressing pad.

Lint roll the mousepad to remove any dust or debris.

Place the mousepad on the blowout paper and cover it with a piece of blowout paper to pre-press for 10 seconds.

Remove the top piece of blowout paper.

Align and secure the transfer sheet face down on the sublimation blank. Using **heat-resistant tape, secure the print to the blank.**

Place a piece of blowout paper on top of the transfer sheet.

Press according to the time indicated in the chart below.

Allow to cool before removing from press then remove the transfer sheet.

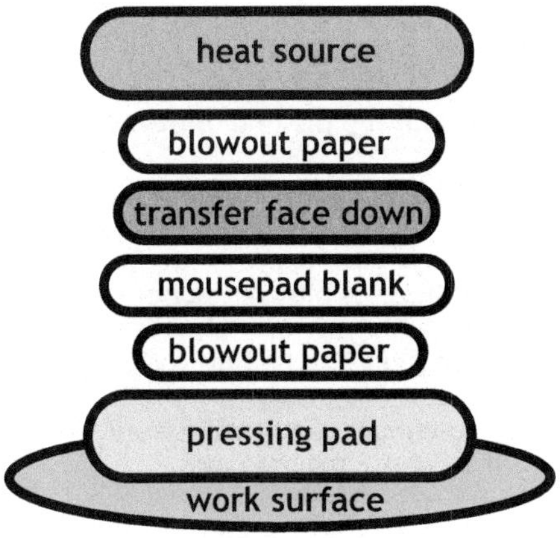

heat source
blowout paper
transfer face down
mousepad blank
blowout paper
pressing pad
work surface

COOK TIMES
Here are typical times you can use as a starting point. Always check the manufacturer's instructions for time and temperature, when available.

your favorite settings

Traditional Heat Press	AutoPress	EasyPress	Mini Press	
400°F / 204°C	400°F / 204°C	385°F / 196°C	High	
45-60 seconds	45 seconds	35 seconds	70 seconds	
40 psi (medium pressure)	Auto pressure	Light pressure	Light pressure	

TIPS & TRICKS
✗ Don't remove your sublimation transfer sheet for at least 10 seconds so it can cool down without ghosting.
✓ If you are having ghosting issues, decrease the temp to 350°F / 177°C and press for 90 seconds.
✓ After pressing neoprene, you may experience cupping or curling of the blank. Place the blank between two heavy objects to help regain shape and flatten the blank.
✓ After Care: Wash in cold water with mild detergent, no bleach, no fabric softener, tumble dry low.

DRINK SLEEVES NEOPRENE

ALSO: Coffee cup sleeves and can coolers

This recipe is for a sublimation-ready neoprene drink sleeve.

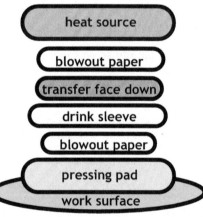

INGREDIENTS
☐ Sublimation blank
☐ Blowout paper (four sheets)
☐ Heat-resistant tape
☐ Sublimation transfers (print/sheet)

EQUIPMENT
☐ Lint roller
☐ Flat heat source such as a heat press

PREPARATION

Start with a drink sleeve sublimation blank.

Pre-heat your flat heat press to the temperature shown in the chart below.

Trim the edges of your sublimation print so it goes just beyond the sublimation blank surface edge. If you use a pre-sewn blank, you will have a seam at the stitched area, so position the seam to the side edge(s) of the blank.

Place a piece of blowout paper (I recommend white cardstock or butcher paper) on the pressing pad.

Place your sublimation blank with a piece of blowout paper on top.

Pre-press for 10 seconds.

Remove the top piece of blowout paper.

Align your sublimation print to one side of the sublimation blank, and secure it with heat-resistant tape.

Place a piece of blowout paper on top of the sublimation print.

Press according to the time indicated in the chart below.

Allow to cool or use heat-resistant gloves to remove the sublimation print and the blank from the press.

Repeat these steps, except for pre-pressing to remove mositure, for the second side of the sublimation blank.

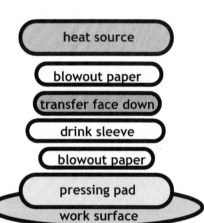

heat source

blowout paper

transfer face down

drink sleeve

blowout paper

pressing pad

work surface

COOK TIMES
Here are typical times you can use as a starting point. Always check the manufacturer's instructions for time and temperature, when available.

your favorite settings

Traditional Heat Press	AutoPress	EasyPress	Mini Press	
400°F / 204°C	400°F / 204°C	385°F / 196°C	High	
45 seconds	45 seconds	40 seconds	70 seconds	
40 psi (medium pressure)	Auto pressure	Light pressure	Light pressure	

TIPS & TRICKS
✗ Don't remove your sublimation transfer for at least 10 seconds to prevent ghosting.
✓ To avoid curling after sublimation, place your blank in between two heavy objects to cool.
✓ Make sure that you work in a space with proper ventilation, as neoprene can let off a strong rubber smell during sublimating.

LUNCHBAGS NEOPRENE

ALSO: Laptop cases and mini-lunch totes

This recipe is for a neoprene lunch bag sublimation blank. These bags are typically 11.5 inches by 6.5 inches and are sublimatable on both sides.

INGREDIENTS

☐ Sublimation lunch bag blank
☐ Blowout paper (5 sheets)
☐ Heat-resistant tape
☐ Sublimation transfers (print/sheet)

EQUIPMENT

☐ Lint roller
☐ Flat heat source such as a heat press

PREPARATION

Start with a sublimation lunch bag blank.

Pre-heat your flat heat press to the temperature shown in the chart below.

Trim the edges of your sublimation transfer to exceed the edge of the sublimation blank.

Use a **lint roller** on the blank to remove any dust and debris.

Pre-press the sublimation blank between two sheets of blowout paper (I recommend white cardstock or butcher paper) for 10 seconds.

Remove the top piece of blowout paper and align the sublimation transfer sheet face down on top of the blank.

Secure with **heat-resistant tape.**

Place a clean piece of blowout paper on top of the transfer sheet.

Press according to the chart below.

Allow to cool before removing from the pressing area, or use heat-resistant gloves to remove.

Repeat the steps, except the pre-press to remove moisture, with the second side of the sublimation blank.

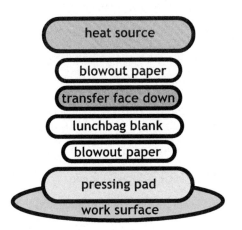

COOK TIMES

Here are typical times you can use as a starting point. Always check the manufacturer's instructions for time and temperature, when available.

your favorite settings

Traditional Heat Press	AutoPress	EasyPress	Mini Press	
400°F / 204°C	400°F / 204°C	385°F / 140°C	High	
60 seconds	60 seconds	35 seconds	70 seconds	
40 psi (medium pressure)	Auto pressure	Light pressure	Light pressure	

TIPS & TRICKS

× Don't remove your sublimation transfer sheet for at least 10 seconds so it can cool down without ghosting.
✓ To prevent the sublimation ink from bleeding through, place a sheet of blowout paper inside the lunchbag.

CHAPSTICK HOLDERS
NEOPRENE
ALSO: Hand sanitizer holders, coin purses

This recipe is for a neoprene sublimation-ready chapstick holder blank. These blanks come in a variety of shapes and sizes, and both sides of the blank are sublimatable.

INGREDIENTS
☐ Chapstick holder sublimation blank
☐ Blowout paper (two sheets cut in half)
☐ Heat-resistant tape
☐ Sublimation transfer (print/sheet)

EQUIPMENT
☐ Lint roller
☐ Flat heat source such as a heat press

PREPARATION

Start with a chapstick holder sublimation blank.

Pre-heat your flat heat press to the temperature shown in the chart below.

Trim the edges of your sublimation print so it goes just beyond the sublimation blank surface edge. You will press this item flat and there will be a seam on the sides of the sublimated blank.

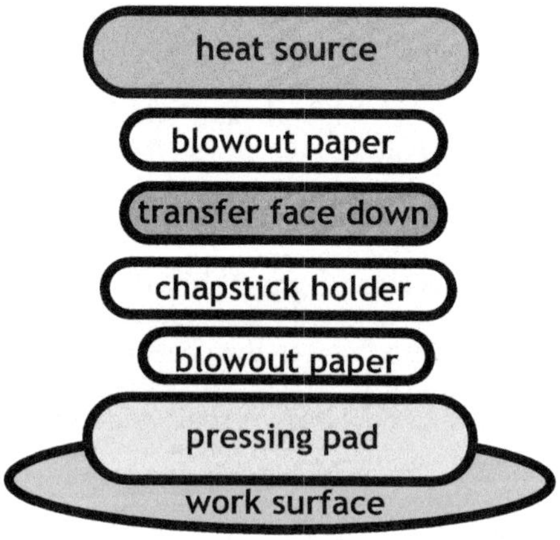

Place a piece of blowout paper on the pressing pad.

Place your sublimation blank with a piece of blowout paper on top.

Pre-press for 10 seconds.

Remove the top piece of blowout paper.

Align your sublimation print to one side of the sublimation blank, and secure it with heat-resistant tape.

Place a piece of blowout paper on top of the sublimation print.

Press according to the time indicated in the chart below.

Allow to cool or use heat-resistant gloves to remove the sublimation print and the blank from the press.

Repeat these steps, except for pre-pressing to remove moisture, for the second side of the sublimation blank.

heat source
blowout paper
transfer face down
chapstick holder
blowout paper
pressing pad
work surface

COOK TIMES
Here are typical times you can use as a starting point. Always check the manufacturer's instructions for time and temperature, when available.

your favorite settings

Traditional Heat Press	AutoPress	EasyPress	Mini Press	
385°F / 196°C	385°F / 196°C	375°F / 190°C	High	
45 seconds	45 seconds	40 seconds	55 seconds	
40 psi (light/medium)	Auto pressure	Light pressure	Light pressure	

TIPS & TRICKS
✓ If your sublimation design is mostly black, you may want to add an extra 10-20 seconds.
✓ Review your design. Outlines and borders can be challenging to line up on these small and oddly-shaped blanks.

CAR COASTERS NEOPRENE

This recipe is for a neoprene car coaster sublimation-ready blank. These blanks typically have one side that is sublimatable.

INGREDIENTS
☐ Car coaster sublimation blank
☐ Blowout paper (two sheets cut in half)
☐ Heat-resistant tape
☐ Sublimation transfer (print/sheet)

EQUIPMENT
☐ Lint roller
☐ Flat heat source such as a heat press

PREPARATION

Start with a car coaster sublimation blank.

Pre-heat your flat heat press to the temperature shown in the chart below.

Trim the edges of your sublimation transfer to exceed the edge of the sublimation blank.

Using a lint roller, remove any dust or debris from the blank.

Pre-press the blank in between two pieces of blowout paper for 10 seconds.

Lint roll the blank a second time before pressing.

Place a piece of clean blowout paper under the blank.

Align and secure the transfer sheet face down on the blank using heat-resistant tape.

Place another piece of blowout paper on top of the transfer sheet.

Press according to the chart below.

Allow to cool or use heat-resistant gloves to remove from the pressing area.

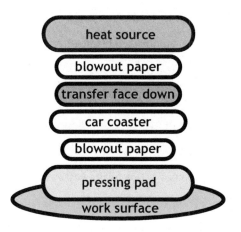

heat source
blowout paper
transfer face down
car coaster
blowout paper
pressing pad
work surface

COOK TIMES
Here are typical times you can use as a starting point. Always check the manufacturer's instructions for time and temperature, when available.

your favorite settings

Traditional Heat Press	AutoPress	EasyPress	Mini Press	
385°F / 196°C	385°F / 196°C	385°F / 196°C	High	
45-55 seconds	50 seconds	40 seconds	70 seconds	
40 psi (medium pressure)	Auto pressure	Light pressure	Light pressure	

TIPS & TRICKS
✓ To prevent curling after sublimation, place the cup coaster between two flat, heavy objects during cooling.
✓ Review your design. Outlines and borders can be challenging to line up on the car coasters.
✓ After Care: Wash in a cold water cycle, tumble dry low heat.

FLIP FLOPS NEOPRENE

This recipe is for the sublimation blank flip flop surface. This product will require some assembly of the sandal straps.

INGREDIENTS
☐ Flip flop sublimation blank
☐ Blowout paper (two sheets)
☐ Heat-resistant tape
☐ Sublimation transfer (print/sheet)

EQUIPMENT
☐ Lint roller
☐ Flat heat source such as a heat press
☐ Needlenose pliers to secure strap to sandal bottom

PREPARATION

Start with the flip flop sublimation blank with the straps removed.

Pre-heat your flat heat press to the temperature shown in the chart below.

Trim your sublimation print to extend just beyond the edge of the blank.

Do not pre-press the flip flop blank. Hover over the heat press surface for 10 seconds to warm the flip flop and help remove any uwanted mositure.

Place a piece of blowout paper (I recommend white cardstock or butcher paper) on your pressing pad.

Place the sublimation blank with the sublimation side facing up on top of the blowout paper.

Align your sublimation transfer sheet onto the blank, and **secure it with heat-resistant tape.**

Place another piece of blowout paper on top.

Press according to the chart below.

Allow to cool or **use heat-resistant gloves** to remove from the press.

Repeat the steps above for the 2nd flip-flop sublimation blank.

Use **needlenose pliers** to push the sandal straps into the sublimated flip-flop bottoms.

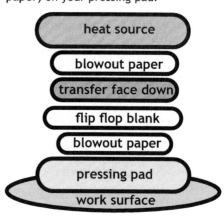

heat source
blowout paper
transfer face down
flip flop blank
blowout paper
pressing pad
work surface

COOK TIMES
Here are typical times you can use as a starting point. Always check the manufacturer's instructions for time and temperature, when available.

your favorite settings

Traditional Heat Press	AutoPress	EasyPress	Mini Press	
400°F / 204°C	400°F / 204°C	385°F / 196°C	High	
30 seconds	30 seconds	40 seconds	55 seconds	
50 psi (Firm pressure)	Auto pressure	Firm pressure	Med pressure	

TIPS & TRICKS
✗ Don't remove your sublimation transfer sheet for at least 10 seconds so it can cool down without ghosting.
✓ Assembling the flip-flop straps will be easier if you lubricate the tool. You can use a non-staining lubrication spray.
✓ After Care: Wash in a cold water cycle with mild detergent, low heat tumble dry.

CHAPTER 12
EVERYTHING ELSE

NOTE

Home sublimation dye printing is still relatively new and there are new and improved materials and processes coming out all the time, which I am evaluating. Early on, I tried some materials and techniques that didn't hold up over time as well as I would like, so I'm going to share those results at the end of this chapter. Those materials include adhesive vinyl, glow-in-the-dark HTV, clear HTV, and clear over white HTV.

T-SHIRTS ALL OR MOSTLY COTTON

Cotton shirts need a little extra help, as cotton alone cannot hold the sublimation ink without washing out. Use HTV (heat transfer vinyl) to retain ink on your cotton shirt!

INGREDIENTS
- ☐ T-shirt made of cotton—darker colors are ok
- ☐ Special HTV such as white glitter, flocked, holographic, or glow in the dark (EasySubli is also an option, but check the manufacturers site for more instructions)
- ☐ Blowout paper (two sheets)
- ☐ Heat-resistant tape
- ☐ Sublimation transfer

EQUIPMENT
- ☐ A way to cut your HTV (cutting machine or craft knife)
- ☐ Lint roller
- ☐ Flat heat source such as a heat press
- ☐ (Optional) T-shirt ruler for placement help
- ☐ (Optional) Pillow or foam for shirts with buttons, seams, zippers, or pockets

PREPARATION

Start with a new shirt for the best results. No need to pre-wash, but if you do, avoid fabric softener.

Pre-heat your flat heat press to the temperature shown in chart below.

Cut and weed your HTV to fit your sublimation transfer using a cutting machine or just a craft knife. It works best if your HTV is a touch smaller than your sublimation transfer so it bleeds to the edges.

LInt roll your shirt to remove any dust and debris.

Fold shirt in half lengthwise so both sides match up, then press for 10 seconds — this pre-heats the shirt to remove moisture and gives you a straight vertical crease for alignment.

Unfold shirt and **slide a piece of blowout paper inside your shirt** (I recommend white cardstock) to keep the sublimation ink from bleeding into the other side of the shirt. A pressing pillow/foam is optional.

Press your HTV to your shirt for 5 seconds only, just enough for it to sitck. Remove the liner while still warm.

Closely trim the edges of your printed sublimation transfer so you can see how to line it up on your HTV. (Not necessary with Infusible Ink sheet.)

Tape all four edges of your sublimation design face down on your HTV already pressed to your shirt, lining up the edges carefully.

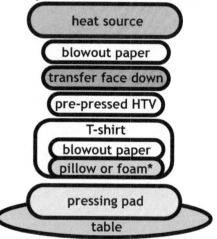

heat source
blowout paper
transfer face down
pre-pressed HTV
T-shirt
blowout paper
pillow or foam*
pressing pad
table

* optional

COOK TIMES
Here are typical times you can use as a starting point. Always check the manufacturer's instructions for time and temperature, when available.

your favorite settings

Traditional Heat Press	AutoPress	Easy Press	Mini Press	
385°F / 196°C	390°F / 199°C	385°F / 196°C	High	
5 + 60-75 seconds	5 + 60-70 seconds	5 + 60-70 seconds	10 + 90 seconds	
40 psi (light/medium)	Auto pressure	Light pressure	Light pressure	

TIPS & TRICKS
✗ Be cautious of pressing onto red and purple shirts, as the dye may bleed through your HTV into your design.
✓ For a tutorial check out jennifermaker.com/how-to-sublimate-on-cotton
✗ Sublimated prints on glow-in-the-dark HTV, white HTV, and clear HTV will blur over time.

CLEAR HTV

EXAMPLE: 100% Cotton T-shirt

This recipe is for clear, matte, or glossy heat transfer vinyl. Clear HTV adheres can be used to sublimate on any color material; however, lighter materials have a better color quality on the finished product. It can be used on other fabrics, wood, glass, and canvas. However, sublimated prints on clear HTV will blur over time.

INGREDIENTS
☐ Clear HTV sheet or roll
☐ 100% Cotton T-Shirt
☐ Blowout paper (three sheets)
☐ Heat-resistant tape
☐ Mirrored sublimation transfer (print/sheet)

EQUIPMENT
☐ Lint roller
☐ Flat heat source such as a heat press
☐ Scissors
☐ (Optional) Vinyl cutting machine
☐ (Optional) Weeding tool
☐ (Optional) T-shirt ruler for placement help

PREPARATION

Start with a new shirt for the best results. No need to pre-wash. **Lint roll** your shirt to remove any dust and debris.

Pre-heat your flat heat press to 385°F / 196°C.

Cut away any excess vinyl material and weed your design. You may choose to use scissors or a cutting machine.

Press the shirt for 10 seconds to remove moisture.

Slide a piece of blowout paper inside your shirt. Optionally, you can also place a pressing pillow under the paper inside your shirt.

Align and place your vinyl onto the shirt. Keep the shiny side up and the matte/textured side down.

Place a piece of blowout paper on top and press to tack down the vinyl for 15 seconds.

Remove the blowout paper and allow it to cool before removing the HTV carrier sheet.

Cut your sublimation transfer print to align with the size and shape of the HTV. You can choose to trim closely with scissors or a cutting machine.

Place another piece of blowout paper below the shirt and a new piece of blowout paper in between the layers of the shirt.

Align your sublimation transfer sheet face down on top of the vinyl and **secure it with heat-resistant tape. Place a piece of blowout paper** on top of the transfer sheet.

Press according to the chart below.

| heat source |
| blowout paper |
| transfer face down |
| HTV |
| T-shirt |
| blowout paper |
| pressing pad |
| work surface |

COOK TIMES
Here are typical times you can use as a starting point. Always check the manufacturer's instructions for time and temperature, when available.

your favorite settings

Traditional Heat Press	AutoPress	EasyPress	Mini Press	
385°F / 196°C	385°F / 196°C	385°F / 196°C	Medium	
30 seconds	30 seconds	30 seconds	40 seconds	
30 psi (light pressure)	Auto pressure	Light pressure	Light pressure	

TIPS & TRICKS
✓ For projects and a tutorial, check out jennifermaker.com/how-to-sublimate-on-cotton/
✗ Sublimated prints on clear HTV will blur over time.

CLEAR OVER WHITE HTV

EXAMPLE: 100% Cotton T-shirt

This recipe uses layers of sublimation paper, clear HTV, and white HTV. Adding a base layer of white vinyl is good for dark-colored shirts. It will provide the opaque background needed for the sublimation design to show up well. However, sublimated prints on clear HTV will blur over time.

INGREDIENTS

☐ Clear HTV sheet or roll
☐ White HTV sheet or roll
☐ 100% Cotton T-Shirt
☐ Blowout paper (three sheets)
☐ Heat-resistant tape
☐ Mirrored sublimation transfer (print/sheet)

EQUIPMENT

☐ Lint roller
☐ Flat heat source such as a heat press
☐ Scissors
☐ (Optional) Vinyl cutting machine
☐ (Optional) Weeding tool
☐ (Optional) T-shirt ruler for placement help

PREPARATION

Start with a new shirt for the best results. No need to pre-wash. **Lint roll** your shirt to remove any dust and debris.

Preheat your flat heat press to 385°F / 196°C

Cut away any excess vinyl material for the clear and white HTV. You may choose to use scissors or a cutting machine. Very closely trim your sublimation transfer print.

Press the shirt for 10 seconds to remove any moisture.

Align and place the white vinyl shiny side up on the shirt. Press for 10 seconds to tack the vinyl down.

Let cool slightly, then remove the carrier sheet.

Align and place the clear vinyl on top of the white vinyl. Cover with a sheet of blowout paper.

Press for 25 seconds.

Wait until completely cooled, then remove the blowout paper and carrier sheet.

Slide a sheet of blowout paper inside the shirt.

Place the sublimation transfer print face down on top of the clear and white vinyl. Align it properly, then secure it in place with heat-resistant tape. Cover everything with another sheet of blowout paper.

Press according to the chart below.

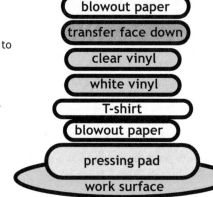

heat source
blowout paper
transfer face down
clear vinyl
white vinyl
T-shirt
blowout paper
pressing pad
work surface

COOK TIMES

Here are typical times you can use as a starting point. Always check the manufacturer's instructions for time and temperature, when available.

your favorite settings

Traditional Heat Press	AutoPress	EasyPress	Mini Press	
385°F / 196°C	385°F / 196°C	385°F / 196°C	Medium	
55 seconds	55 seconds	55 seconds	60 seconds	
50 psi (heavy pressure)	Auto pressure	Heavy pressure	Heavy pressure	

TIPS & TRICKS

✓ For projects and a tutorial, check out jennifermaker.com/how-to-sublimate-on-cotton/
✗ Sublimated prints on clear HTV will blur over time.

ADHESIVE VINYL

GLASS EXAMPLE: Cutting Board

This recipe will use either white adhesive vinyl or transparent adhesive vinyl on a glass surface to create a sublimation ready surface. The end result will be a stained glass effect. Unfortunately, sublimated prints on adhesive vinyl will blur over time.

INGREDIENTS
☐ Dollar tree glass cutting board
☐ White permanent adhesive vinyl -OR-
☐ Transparent adhesive vinyl
☐ Sublimation transfer (print/sheet)
☐ Heat-resistant tape
☐ StandardGrip transfer tape
☐ Blowout paper

EQUIPMENT
☐ Microfiber cloth/Lint-free cloth
☐ Rubbing alcohol
☐ Flat heat source such as a heat press
☐ Heat resistant gloves
☐ Scissors
☐ Cricut scraper
☐ Shallow baking pan
☐ Spray bottle with water and dishsoap
☐ (Optional) Glass window hanging kit

PREPARATION

Prep the glass cutting board by removing the rubber feet and clean both sides of the glass with rubbing alcohol.

Pre-heat your flat press to the temperature shown in the chart below.

Set the cutting board down on a sheet of vinyl and use a pen to trace around the outside edge. Then **cut the vinyl shape with scissors.**

Next, **use the wet method to apply the adhesive vinyl to the smooth side of the cutting board.**

Allow the vinyl and the cutting board to dry completely before placing the sublimation transfer sheet face down on the vinyl.

Use heat-resistant tape to secure the sublimation transfer sheet to the cutting board.

Flip the cutting board over so that the smooth glass is on the top.

Place another piece of blowout paper on top of the cutting board.

Press according to the chart below. If using an EasyPress, press for 90 seconds and then rotate the press 90 degrees and continue pressing for an additional 90 seconds.

Using heat-resistant gloves, set the cutting board aside to cool. **Once cooled, allow the cutting board to soak in a shallow baking pan (or your sink) until the paper releases easily from the cutting board.**

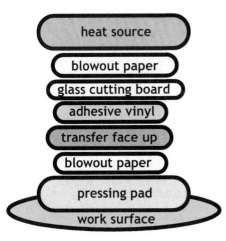

heat source
blowout paper
glass cutting board
adhesive vinyl
transfer face up
blowout paper
pressing pad
work surface

COOK TIMES
Here are typical times you can use as a starting point. Always check the manufacturer's instructions for time and temperature, when available.

your favorite settings

Traditional Heat Press	AutoPress	EasyPress	Mini Press	
385°F / 196°C	385°F / 196°C	385°F / 196°C	High	
120 seconds	120 seconds	90* seconds	120 seconds	
30 psi (Light pressure)	Light pressure	Light pressure	Medium pressure	

TIPS & TRICKS
✓ To review the wet method check out https://jennifermaker.com/how-to-apply-vinyl-with-the-wet-method/
✓ Review the tutorial for this project and the wet application method check out https://www.jennifermaker.com/can-you-sublimate-on-glass/
✗ Sublimated prints on adhesive vinyl will blur over time.
✗ White vinyl will fade faster, so keep your finished piece away from direct sunlight.

GLITTER HTV

EXAMPLE: Dark colored poly-cotton blend make-up bag

Glitter HTV can be used to sublimate on both light and dark colors, allowing you to use a variety of blanks. Glitter HTV will adhere to cotton, poly-blends, canvas, wood, glass, and more.

INGREDIENTS
☐ Glitter HTV sheet or roll
☐ Poly-blend make-up bag
☐ Blowout paper (three sheets)
☐ Heat-resistant tape
☐ Mirrored sublimation transfer (print/sheet)

EQUIPMENT
☐ Lint roller
☐ Flat heat source such as a heat press
☐ Weeding tool
☐ Scissors
☐ (Optional) Cutting machine

PREPARATION

Start with your blank. For our example, we are using a poly-blend dark make-up bag.

Pre-heat your flat heat press to 320°F / 160°C.

Lint-roll your blank to remove any dust and debris, then **pre-press your blank** for 15 seconds to remove any moisture.

Cut away any excess vinyl material and weed your design. You may choose to use scissors or a cutting machine.

Align and place your vinyl onto the blank. You want to keep the shiny side up and the matte/textured side down.

Tack down the vinyl for 10 seconds. Peel the carrier sheet off while it is still warm.

Increase the heat of your press to the temperature listed in the chart below.

Cut your sublimation transfer print to align with the size and shape of the HTV. You can choose to trim closely with scissors or a cutting machine.

Place another piece of blowout paper below the blank.

Align your **sublimation transfer sheet face down** on top of the vinyl and **secure it with heat-resistant tape.**

Place a piece of blowout paper on top of the transfer sheet.

Press according to the chart below. **Remove the transfer sheet while still warm.**

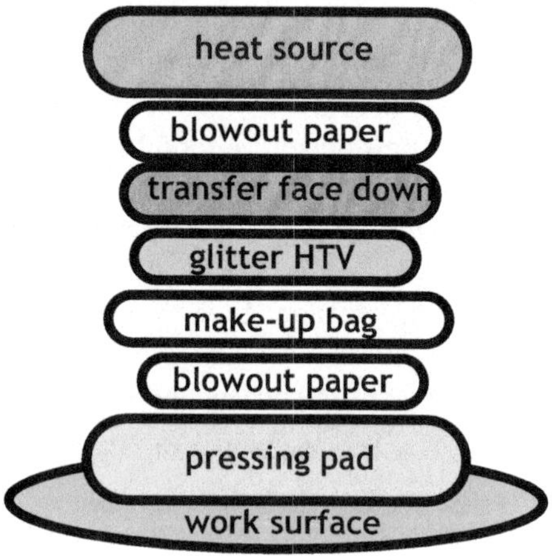

| heat source |
| blowout paper |
| transfer face down |
| glitter HTV |
| make-up bag |
| blowout paper |
| pressing pad |
| work surface |

COOK TIMES
Here are typical times you can use as a starting point. Always check the manufacturer's instructions for time and temperature, when available.

your favorite settings

Traditional Heat Press	AutoPress	EasyPress	Mini Press	
400°F / 204°C	400°F / 204°C	385°F / 196°C	Medium	
35-40 seconds	35-40 seconds	40 seconds	50 seconds	
30 psi (light pressure)	Auto pressure	Light pressure	Light pressure	

TIPS & TRICKS
✗ Don't remove your sublimation transfer sheet for at least 10 seconds so it can cool down without ghosting.
✓ For a tutorial check out jennifermaker.com/how-to-sublimate-on-cotton/

HOLOGRAPHIC HTV

EXAMPLE: Dark polyester car flag

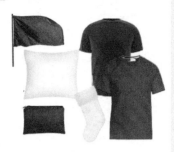

Holographic HTV can be applied to dark or light colors to help create a color-changing illusion on your sublimation. Holographic HTV will adhere to polyester, cotton, poly-cotton blends, and some lycra and spandex materials.

INGREDIENTS
☐ Holographic HTV sheet or roll
☐ Polyester car flag
☐ Blowout paper (three sheets)
☐ Heat-resistant tape
☐ Mirrored sublimation transfer (print/sheet)

EQUIPMENT
☐ Lint roller
☐ Flat heat source such as a heat press
☐ Scissors
☐ Weeding tool
☐ (Optional) Cutting machine

PREPARATION

Start with your blank. For our example, we are using a dark polyester car flag.

Pre-heat your flat heat press to 320°F / 160°C.

Lint roll your blank to remove dust and debis, then **pre-press your blank** for 10 seconds to remove any moisture.

Cut away any excess vinyl material and weed your design if needed. You may choose to use scissors or a cutting machine.

Align and place your vinyl onto the blank. You want to keep the shiny side up and the matte/textured side down.

Place a piece of blowout paper on top and press to tack down the vinyl for 10 seconds. **Remove the blowout paper** and allow it to cool before removing the carrier sheet.

Increase the heat of your press to the temperature listed in the chart below.

Cut your sublimation transfer print to align with the size and shape of the HTV. You can choose to trim closely with scissors or a cutting machine.

Place another piece of blowout paper below the blank.

Align your **sublimation transfer sheet face down** on top of the vinyl and **secure it with heat-resistant tape.**

Place a piece of blowout paper on top of the transfer sheet.

Press according to the chart below. Carefully remove the transfer sheet while still warm.

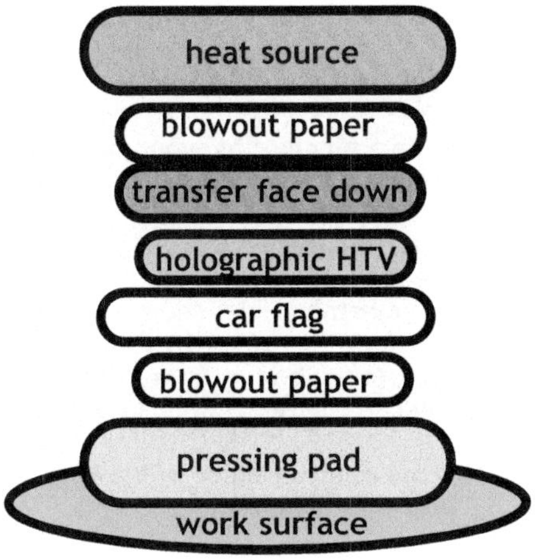

| heat source |
| blowout paper |
| transfer face down |
| holographic HTV |
| car flag |
| blowout paper |
| pressing pad |
| work surface |

COOK TIMES
Here are typical times you can use as a starting point. Always check the manufacturer's instructions for time and temperature, when available.

your favorite settings

Traditional Heat Press	AutoPress	EasyPress	Mini Press	
380°F / 193°C	380°F / 193°C	380°F / 193°C	High	
40 seconds	40 seconds	40 seconds	50 seconds	
30 psi (light)	Auto pressure	Light pressure	Light pressure	

TIPS & TRICKS
✓ For a tutorial check out jennifermaker.com/how-to-sublimate-on-cotton/

GLOW IN THE DARK HTV

EXAMPLE: 100% cotton sweatshirt

Glow in the Dark HTV is a polyurethane-based heat transfer material that can glow in the dark. Glow in the Dark HTV can adhere to a variety of textile materials, including leather. However, sublimated prints on glow-in-the-dark HTV will blur over time.

INGREDIENTS
☐ Glow in the dark HTV sheet or roll
☐ 100% Cotton Sweatshirt
☐ Blowout paper (three sheets)
☐ Heat-resistant tape
☐ Mirrored sublimation transfer (print/sheet)

EQUIPMENT
☐ Lint roller
☐ Flat heat source such as a heat press
☐ (Optional) T-shirt ruler for placement help
☐ (Optional) Pillow or foam for shirts with buttons, seams, zippers, or pockets

PREPARATION

Start with a new shirt for the best results. No need to pre-wash. **Lint roll** sweatshirt to remove any dust and debris.

Pre-heat your flat heat press to the temperature shown in the chart below.

Cut away any excess vinyl material and weed your design. You may choose to use scissors or a cutting machine.

Press shirt for 10 seconds to eliminate moisture.

Slide a piece of blowout paper inside your sweatshirt. Optionally, you can also place a pressing pillow under the paper inside your sweatshirt.

Align and place your vinyl onto the shirt. You want to keep the shiny side up and the matte/textured side down. **Press to tack down the vinyl for 10 seconds.** Remove the carrier sheet while warm.

Cut your sublimation transfer print to align with the size and shape of the HTV. You can choose to trim closely with scissors or a cutting machine.

Place another piece of blowout paper below the sweatshirt **and a new piece of blowout paper** in between the layers of the sweatshirt.

Align your sublimation transfer sheet face down on top of the vinyl and secure it with heat-resistant tape.

Place a piece of blowout paper on top of the transfer sheet.

Press according to the chart below.

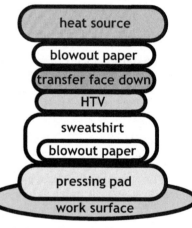

heat source
blowout paper
transfer face down
HTV
sweatshirt
blowout paper
pressing pad
work surface

COOK TIMES

Here are typical times you can use as a starting point. Always check the manufacturer's instructions for time and temperature, when available.

your favorite settings

Traditional Heat Press	AutoPress	EasyPress	Mini Press	
380°F / 193°C	380°F / 193°C	380°F / 193°C	High	
70 seconds	70 seconds	70 seconds	80 seconds	
30 psi (light)	Auto pressure	Light pressure	Light pressure	

TIPS & TRICKS
✓ For projects and tutorials, check out jennifermaker.com/how-to-sublimate-on-cotton/
✗ Sublimated prints on glow-in-the-dark HTV will blur over time.

EASYSUBLI

EXAMPLE: Colored cotton t-shirt

Siser EasySubli is designed to be used with sublimation and comes with heat-resistant mask transfer tape. EasySubli can be used on almost any blank that accepts vinyl and HTV.

INGREDIENTS
☐ Blank cotton t-shirt
☐ Siser EasySubli (one sheet)
☐ Blowout paper (two sheets)
☐ Heat-resistant tape
☐ Sublimation transfer (print/sheet)
☐ (Optional) EasySubli mask transfer tape

EQUIPMENT
☐ Lint roller
☐ Flat heat source such as a heat press
☐ (Optional) T-shirt ruler for placement help
☐ (Optional) Pillow or foam for shirts with buttons, seams, zippers, or pockets

PREPARATION

Start with a new shirt for the best results. No need to pre-wash, but if you do, avoid fabric softener. Use a lint roller to clean the surface of your shirt.

Pre-heat your flat heat press to the temperature shown in the chart below.

Lay your shirt on the pressing pad. **Press for 10 seconds to eliminate any moisture.**

Cut your print-then-cut sublimation transfer and EasySubli shape. Make sure the transfer is mirrored, but the EasySubli shape is not. Weed the transfer. Weed and closely trim the EasySubli shape.

Lay the EasySubli shape with the carrier sheet facing down on your work surface. Peel the mask transfer tape from the backing and apply it to the EasySubli shape. Use a scraper to smooth out any bubbles and creases.

Peel the EasySubli shape away from the carrier sheet. The mask is not necessary if your shape is solid and not complicated.

Place a sheet of blowout paper (I recommend cardstock) inside the shirt. **Place the EasySubli shape on the shirt face down.** Cover with blowout paper. Press for 5 seconds to tack the EasySubli to the shirt. Remove the blowout paper. If using a mask, peel the it off while still warm.

Place the sublimation transfer face down on the EasySubli, making sure it is aligned properly. Secure in place with heat-resistant tape. Cover with another sheet of blowout paper.

Press according to the chart below. Pull the transfer sheet while still warm.

| heat source |
| blowout paper |
| transfer face down |
| EasySubli face down |
| T-shirt |
| blowout paper |
| pillow or foam* |
| pressing pad |
| work surface |

* optional

COOK TIMES
Here are typical times you can use as a starting point. Always check the manufacturer's instructions for time and temperature, when available.

your favorite settings

Traditional Heat Press	AutoPress	EasyPress	Mini Press	
385°F / 196°C	385°F / 196°C	385°F / 196°C	High	
40 seconds	40 seconds	40 seconds	50 seconds	
30 psi (light pressure)	Auto pressure	Light pressure	Light pressure	

TIPS & TRICKS
✗ Don't remove your sublimation transfer sheet for at least 10 seconds so it can cool down without ghosting.
✓ For a tutorial check out *jennifermaker.com/how-to-sublimate-on-cotton/*

EASYCOLOR DTV

EXAMPLE: Colored cotton t-shirt

Siser EasyColor DTV (Direct-to-Vinyl) is not true sublimation, but instead is a printable heat-transfer vinyl that uses inkjet printer ink to create a similar effect.

INGREDIENTS
☐ Blank cotton shirt
☐ Siser EasyColor DTV (one sheet)
☐ EasyColor mask transfer tape (one sheet)
☐ Blowout paper (two sheets)
☐ Heat-resistant tape

EQUIPMENT
☐ Lint roller
☐ Flat heat source such as a heat press
☐ (Optional) T-shirt ruler for placement help
☐ (Optional) Pillow or foam for shirts with buttons, seams, zippers, or pockets

PREPARATION

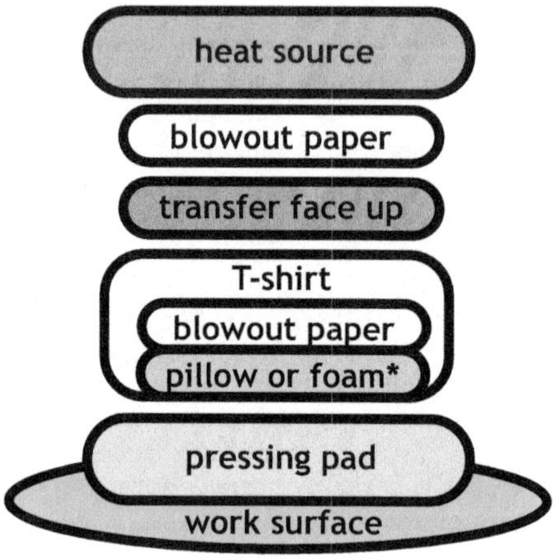

Start with a new shirt for the best results. No need to pre-wash, but if you do, avoid fabric softener. Use a lint roller to clean the surface of your shirt.

Pre-heat your flat heat press to the temperature shown in the chart below.

Place a sheet of blowout paper (I recommend white cardstock or butcher paper) on the pressing pad. Lay your shirt on it and cover it with another sheet of blowout paper. **Press for 10 seconds to eliminate any moisture.**

Print and cut your print-then-cut design on a sheet of EasyColor DTV using an inkjet printer, **taking care to make sure you print on the white side of the sheet.**

Weed and trim the transfer.

Place a sheet of EasySubli mask transfer tape over the face of the transfer. Use a scraper to work out any creases and bubbles.

Use the mask transfer tape to **peel the design transfer away from the carrier sheet.**

Place the transfer face up with the mask on top of the shirt. Cover with a sheet of butcher paper.

Press according to the chart below. Pull the transfer sheet while still hot, immediately after pressing.

heat source
blowout paper
transfer face up
T-shirt
blowout paper
pillow or foam*
pressing pad
work surface

* optional

COOK TIMES
Here are typical times you can use as a starting point. Always check the manufacturer's instructions for time and temperature, when available.

your favorite settings

Traditional Heat Press	AutoPress	EasyPress	Mini Press	
310°F / 154°C	310°F / 154°C	310°F / 154°C	Medium	
15 seconds	15 seconds	15 seconds	20 seconds	
30 psi (light pressure)	Auto pressure	Light pressure	Light pressure	

TIPS & TRICKS
✗ Do not mirror your design.
✓ Shaking your shirt immediately after lifting off the transfer sheet can help remove pressing lines.
✓ After Care: Wash inside out in cold water with mild detergent, no bleach, no fabric softener, and tumble dry low.

DTF & TRANSFER POWDER

EXAMPLE: Light-colored cotton t-shirt

DTF (direct-to-film) is a semi-transparent sheet of film. Transfer powder is a powder adhesive that helps the sublimation ink transfer to a blank. These can be used on many blanks. CAUTION: ALWAYS use PPE and powder that is approved as safe to use.

INGREDIENTS
- ☐ Blank cotton shirt
- ☐ DTF transfer film
- ☐ Hot melt adhesive transfer powder
- ☐ Blowout paper (two sheets)
- ☐ Heat-resistant tape
- ☐ Sublimation transfer (print/sheet)

EQUIPMENT
- ☐ Lint roller
- ☐ Flat heat source such as a heat press
- ☐ (Optional) T-shirt ruler for placement help
- ☐ (Optional) Pillow or foam for shirts with buttons, seams, zippers, or pockets

PREPARATION

Start with a new shirt for the best results. Use a lint roller to clean your shirt.

Pre-heat your flat heat press to the temperature shown in the chart below.

Lay your shirt on the pressing pad and pr**e-press for 10 seconds to eliminate any moisture.**

Tape the DTF transfer film to a sheet of copy paper on the top edge with the shiny side of the transfer film touching the copy paper. Place them in your printer so it takes the taped end first and prints on the film. **Print your transfer. Immediately move to the next step, because you must put the powder on as soon as it prints while the ink is still a little wet. This is very important.**

Place a sheet of blowout paper (I recommend white cardstock or butcher paper) on your work surface. Lay the transfer face up on the blowout paper. **Using a scoop, immediately sprinkle the transfer powder over the design until it is covered. Do this while the ink is still fresh and warm.**

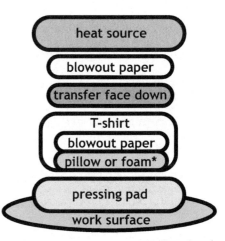

heat source
blowout paper
transfer face down
T-shirt
blowout paper
pillow or foam*
pressing pad
work surface

* optional

Lift the transfer up and allow the extra powder to fall onto the blowout paper. Lightly tap the transfer on the blowout paper. Using gloves, lightly brush off any extra powder around your design.

Lay the transfer (still taped to the copy paper) on the pressing mat. **Hover your heat press closely over the transfer so the powder begins to melt. Do this for 10 seconds. Take care not to touch the transfer with the heat press.**

Closely trim the transfer and detach it from the copy paper. **Slide a piece of blowout paper inside your shirt.** Place the shirt on the pressing pad. Place the transfer face down on the shirt and secure it in place with heat-resistant transfer tape. Place another sheet of blowout paper on top.

Press according to the chart below. Pull the transfer sheet after it has cooled completely.

COOK TIMES

Here are typical times you can use as a starting point. Always check the manufacturer's instructions for time and temperature, when available.

your favorite settings

Traditional Heat Press	AutoPress	EasyPress	Mini Press	
385°F / 196°C	385°F / 196°C	385°F / 196°C	High	
40 seconds	40 seconds	40 seconds	50 seconds	
30 psi (light pressure)	Auto pressure	Light pressure	Light pressure	

TIPS & TRICKS
✓ For a tutorial check out jennifermaker.com/dtf-t-shirt-printing-on-cotton-sublimation/
✓ Important: Use gloves, a mask, and protective glasses when working with transfer powder. Also protect your equipment.

LAMINATION SHEETS
Example: Galvanized metal sign

Thermal lamination sheets adhere to non-sublimation-coated blanks using heat. Popular brands include Scotch, Fellowes, and Swingline. Thermal lamination sheets can be used on rigid surfaces such as wood, metal, canvas, tile, ceramic, glass, and more.

INGREDIENTS
☐ Galvanized metal sign
☐ Thermal laminating sheet
☐ Blowout paper (two sheets)
☐ Heat-resistant tape
☐ Sublimation transfer (print/sheet)

EQUIPMENT
☐ Lint roller
☐ Flat heat source such as a heat press
☐ Pen
☐ (Optional) Ruler for measuring

PREPARATION

Pre-heat your flat heat press to the temperature shown in the chart below.

Closely trim the edges of your printed sublimation transfer.

Lay a single lamination sheet on your work surface. **Place the metal sign on top of it and trace around it with a pen.** Cut the lamination sheet.

Place the metal sign face up on your work surface, then lay the lamination sheet shiny side up on top. Secure it in place with heat-resistant tape.

Place a sheet of blowout paper on your pressing pad. **Lay the metal sign with lamination sheet face up.** Place another sheet of blowout paper on top. Heat for 15-20 seconds to tack the laminate onto the metal sign. Let cool.

Place the metal sign with the laminate face up on your work surface. Lay your sublimation transfer face down on top of the sign. Align it and then secure it with heat-resistant tape.

Place a sheet of blowout paper on your pressing pad. **Lay the metal sign with sublimation transfer side up.** Place another sheet of blowout paper on top.

Press according to the chart below. Pull the transfer sheet while still warm.

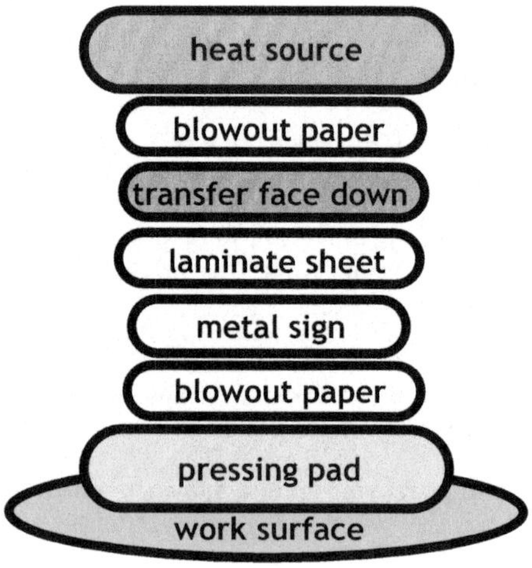

heat source
blowout paper
transfer face down
laminate sheet
metal sign
blowout paper
pressing pad
work surface

COOK TIMES
Here are typical times you can use as a starting point. Always check the manufacturer's instructions for time and temperature, when available.

your favorite settings

Traditional Heat Press	AutoPress	EasyPress	Mini Press	
400°F / 204°C	400°F / 204°C	400°F / 204°C	400°F / 204°C	
60 seconds	60 seconds	60 seconds	70 seconds	
30 psi (light pressure)	Light pressure	Light pressure	Light pressure	

TIPS & TRICKS
✗ Don't remove your sublimation transfer sheet for at least 10 seconds so it can cool down without ghosting.
✓ If using a thermal laminating pouch, cut it open and use only a single side.
✓ For a tutorial using lamination check out *jennifermaker.com/dollar-tree-sublimation-ideas/*

LAMINATE SHEET

GLASS EXAMPLE: Cutting Board

This recipe will use the application of a laminate sheet on a glass cutting board to create a sublimation ready surface. The end result will be a stained glass effect.

INGREDIENTS
☐ Glass cutting board
☐ Clear thermal laminating pouch
☐ Sublimation transfer (print/sheet)
☐ Heat-resistant tape
☐ Blowout paper

EQUIPMENT
☐ Rubbing alcohol
☐ Lint-free cloth
☐ Flat heat source such as a heat press
☐ Heat-resistant gloves
☐ Pen/Pencil and ruler
☐ Scissors
☐ (Optional) Glass window hanging kit

PREPARATION

Prep the glass cutting board by removing the rubber feet and clean both sides of the glass with rubbing alcohol.

Pre-heat your flat press to the temperature shown in the chart below.

Separate the laminate pouch into two pieces, trace the cutting board on one of the pieces with a pencil. **Cut the laminate** to the board's shape.

Place a piece of blowout paper on your pressing pad, then place the glass cutting board textured side down on top of the blowout paper.

Place the laminate with the shiny side up on top of the smooth side of the cutting board. **Use heat-resistant tape to secure in place.**

Place a piece of blowout paper on top of the laminate sheet.

Once the **press reaches the correct temperature**, press the project for 60 seconds to tack the laminate down.

The glass cutting board will be very hot! Only handle it while wearing heat-resistant gloves.

When the laminated cutting board is cool to the touch, it's time to press your design.

Place the sublimation image face up and lay the cutting board laminated side down on top of the image. Make sure everything is centered and secure it with heat-resistant tape around the edge of the cutting board.

Cover your pressing pad with a sheet of blowout paper and place the cutting board textured side down on top of the blowout paper. Place a piece of blowout paper on top of the sublimation transfer sheet.

Press according to the chart below. Pull the transfer sheet while still warm. If using an EasyPress you will press for 60 seconds and then rotate the press 90 degrees and press for an additional 60 seconds.

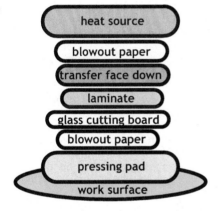

COOK TIMES
Here are typical times you can use as a starting point. Always check the manufacturer's instructions for time and temperature, when available.

your favorite settings

Traditional Heat Press	AutoPress	EasyPress	Mini Press	
400°F / 204°C	400°F / 204°C	400°F / 204°C	High	
60 seconds	60 seconds	60 seconds	60 seconds	
30 psi (Light pressure)	Light pressure	Light pressure	Medium pressure	

TIPS & TRICKS
✓ Review the tutorial for this project at https://www.jennifermaker.com/can-you-sublimate-on-glass/

SUBLIMATION SPRAY

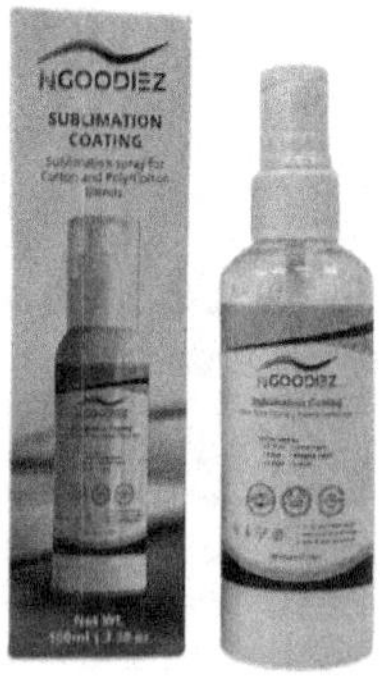

EXAMPLE: Colored cotton t-shirt

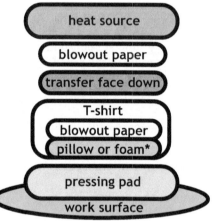

Sublimation spray comes in cans or bottles and can be used to coat almost any surface for sublimation. Spray for fabrics is different than spray for hard surfaces, so take care to choose the correct spray for your blank.

INGREDIENTS
☐ Cotton shirt
☐ Sublimation spray
☐ Blowout paper (two sheets)
☐ Heat-resistant tape
☐ Sublimation transfer (print/sheet)

EQUIPMENT
☐ Lint roller
☐ Foam roller
☐ Flat heat source such as a heat press
☐ (Optional) T-shirt ruler for placement help
☐ (Optional) Pillow or foam for shirts with buttons, seams, zippers, or pockets

PREPARATION

Start with a new shirt for the best results. No need to pre-wash, but if you do, avoid fabric softener. Use a lint roller to clean the surface of your shirt.

Pre-heat your flat heat press to the temperature shown in the chart below.

Lay blowout paper on your work surface. Place the shirt on the blowout paper.

Spray an even coat of sublimation spray over the area you want to sublimate on the shirt.

Use a foam roller to roll over the area to spread the spray evenly.

Let the shirt dry for one hour or until it is dry to the touch.

Pre-press the shirt for 10 seconds to eliminate any moisture.

Slide another sheet of blowout paper into the shirt to prevent any ink from bleeding through.

Place the sublimation transfer face down on the shirt. Secure it in place with heat-resistant tape. Cover with a sheet of blowout paper.

Press according to the chart below. Pull the transfer sheet while still warm.

heat source
blowout paper
transfer face down
T-shirt
blowout paper
pillow or foam*
pressing pad
work surface

* optional

COOK TIMES
Here are typical times you can use as a starting point. Always check the manufacturer's instructions for time and temperature, when available.

your favorite settings

Traditional Heat Press	AutoPress	EasyPress	Mini Press	
380°F / 193°C	380°F / 193°C	380°F / 193°C	High	
35 seconds	35 seconds	35 seconds	40 seconds	
30 psi (light pressure)	Auto pressure	Light pressure	Light pressure	

TIPS & TRICKS
✓ Remember to mirror your design.
✓ Shake the sublimation spray bottle or can well before applying it to your blank surface.
✗ Don't remove your sublimation transfer sheet for at least 10 seconds so it can cool down without ghosting.
✓ Shaking your shirt immediately after lifting off the transfer sheet can help remove pressing lines.

POLY GLOSS

EXAMPLE: Ceramic tile

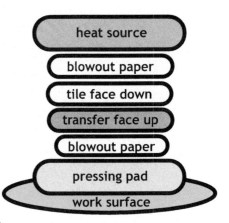

PolyGloss can be used to make some surfaces, such as a ceramic tile, sublimation-ready.

INGREDIENTS
☐ Ceramic tile
☐ Blowout paper (two sheets)
☐ Heat-resistant tape
☐ Sublimation transfer (print/sheet)
☐ Poly Gloss kit

EQUIPMENT
☐ Rubbing alcohol
☐ Lint-free cloth
☐ Heat-resistant gloves
☐ Nylon paint brush
☐ Silicone cooking mat
☐ Flat heat source such as a heat press
☐ Oven

PREPARATION

Clean the tile with alcohol and a lint-free cloth. Let dry. Cover your work area with butcher paper. Place the tile face up on the work surface.

Mix the 2-part PolyGloss polyester resin according to the manufacturer's directions (1 milliliter catalyst to 1 ounce PolyGloss).

Pour a small amount of mixed PolyGloss onto the surface of the tile.

Use the nylon brush to spread the PolyGloss across the entire surface of the tile. Any bubbles in the coating will pop as the PolyGloss dries.

Allow the PolyGloss to dry thoroughly to the touch, approximately 2-6 hours.

Once the PolyGloss coating on the tile is dry and free of surface issues, heat the tile in an oven to cure the coating. For a convection oven, bake at 300°F / 148°C for 22 minutes. For a standard kitchen oven, bake at 340°F /171°C for 22 minutes.

Using heat-resistant gloves, remove the tile from the oven and sit it on a cooling rack to cool approximately 15-20 minutes.

Pre-heat your heat press to 400°F (204°C). Place a piece of blowout paper onto a pressing pad, then place the sublimation transfer/print face up on top of the cardstock.

Place the tile face down on top of the sublimation transfer/print, then secure in place using heat-resistant tape.

Drape a silicone cooking mat over the tile to help heat the tile evenly. Press according to the chart below.

Using heat-resistant gloves, remove the silicone cover, then wait approximately 15 seconds before removing the tile from the sublimation paper. Allow the tile to cool thoroughly.

Diagram (top to bottom):
- heat source
- blowout paper
- tile face down
- transfer face up
- blowout paper
- pressing pad
- work surface

COOK TIMES

Here are typical times you can use as a starting point. Always check the manufacturer's instructions for time and temperature, when available.

your favorite settings

Traditional Heat Press	AutoPress	EasyPress	Mini Press	
400°F / 204°C	400°F / 204°C	400°F / 204°C	High	
10 minutes	10 minutes	10 minutes	10 minutes	
50 psi (Firm pressure)	Auto pressure	Firm pressure	Firm pressure	

TIPS & TRICKS

✓ If you are in a dry environment, cover the tile with a plastic container for about 10 minutes to help slow the drying process and give the bubbles more time to disappear.
✓ To help prevent fading, apply a thin layer of clear acrylic spray to the tile after it has cooled.

SUBLIMATION ON VINYL ISSUES

Home sublimation dye printing is still relatively new and I am continually learning about processes, just like you! Unfortunately, some of the materials in this chapter just don't hold up well over time, and the sublimated designs blur as time passes. I have found that adhesive vinyl, glow-in-the-dark HTV, and clear HTV suffer from this issue. These materials might still be useful in the short-term, but you won't want to use them on projects that you plan to display or wear for a long time. Below, you will see what happened to the sublimated designs on those vinyls over time.

White HTV

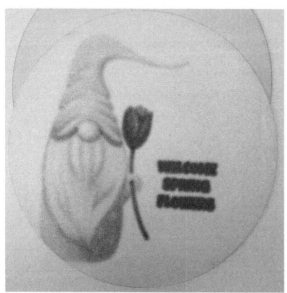

Clear HTV (over white paint)

Glow-in-the-Dark HTV

BEYOND THE RECIPES

WORKSHEETS & NOTES

These worksheets help you track important things for your projects.

Feel free to make as many copies of them as you need!

PROJECT IDEA:

What Is It: _____

Where I Heard About It: _____

Do I Have an design? ❑ (Saved To: _____ File Name: _____)

Is it in Design Space or Canva? ❑ (Name: _____)

Saved Where? ❑ Cloud ❑ _____

Notes For This Project: _____

_____

_____

_____

_____

Tools/Accessories I Need:

_____ ❑ own it (location: _____) ❑ need it (from: _____)

_____ ❑ own it (location: _____) ❑ need it (from: _____)

_____ ❑ own it (location: _____) ❑ need it (from: _____)

_____ ❑ own it (location: _____) ❑ need it (from: _____)

_____ ❑ own it (location: _____) ❑ need it (from: _____)

Materials/Supplies I Need:

_____ ❑ have it (location: _____) ❑ need it (from: _____)

_____ ❑ have it (location: _____) ❑ need it (from: _____)

_____ ❑ have it (location: _____) ❑ need it (from: _____)

_____ ❑ have it (location: _____) ❑ need it (from: _____)

_____ ❑ have it (location: _____) ❑ need it (from: _____)

Shopping List:

❑ _____   ❑ _____

❑ _____   ❑ _____

❑ _____   ❑ _____

❑ _____   ❑ _____

COOK TIMES

Temperature				
Time				
Pressure				

PROJECT NOTES:

Name: _____

Where I Found the Design: _____

Font(s) Used: _____

Saved as PNG? ❏ (Saved To: _____ File Name: _____)

Saved Where? ❏ Cloud ❏ _____

Notes For This Project: _____

_____

_____

Best Material Settings: _____

Materials Used: _____

_____

_____

_____

Techniques Used: _____

_____

_____

_____

Supplies and Tools Used: _____

_____

_____

_____

Special Notes: _____

_____

_____

_____

_____

_____

_____

_____

_____

MY FAVORITE WEB SITES

Where I Find Great Designs: _____

URL: _____ Login/Password: _____
URL: _____ Login/Password: _____
URL: _____ Login/Password: _____
URL: _____ Login/Password: _____
URL: _____ Login/Password: _____
URL: _____ Login/Password: _____
URL: _____ Login/Password: _____
URL: _____ Login/Password: _____
URL: _____ Login/Password: _____

Where I Find Great Fonts: _____

URL: _____ Login/Password: _____
URL: _____ Login/Password: _____
URL: _____ Login/Password: _____
URL: _____ Login/Password: _____
URL: _____ Login/Password: _____
URL: _____ Login/Password: _____
URL: _____ Login/Password: _____
URL: _____ Login/Password: _____
URL: _____ Login/Password: _____
URL: _____ Login/Password: _____
URL: _____ Login/Password: _____
URL: _____ Login/Password: _____

Where I Find Great Tutorials: _____

URL: _____ Login/Password: _____
URL: _____ Login/Password: _____
URL: _____ Login/Password: _____
URL: _____ Login/Password: _____
URL: _____ Login/Password: _____
URL: _____ Login/Password: _____
URL: _____ Login/Password: _____
URL: _____ Login/Password: _____
URL: _____ Login/Password: _____

MY FAVORITE BRANDS

Sublimation Printer

* _____

Inkjet Printer for Print Then Cut

* _____

Sublimation Ink Brand

* _____

ICC Printing Profiles

* _____
* _____
* _____

Sublimation Paper Brands & Types

* _____
* _____
* _____
* _____

Blowout Paper Brands & Types

* _____
* _____
* _____
* _____

Sublimation Blanks

* _____
* _____
* _____
* _____
* _____
* _____
* _____

MY FILE ORGANIZATION

Where I Save My Files: _____

_____

Organized By: ❑ Alphabetical ❑ Designer ❑ Type/Format ❑ Date

My File Folder Structure:

📁 _____

📁 _____

📁 _____

📁 _____

📁 _____

📁 _____

📁 _____

📁 _____

📁 _____

📁 _____

📁 _____

📁 _____

📁 _____

Notes: _____

_____

_____

_____

_____

_____

INDEX

SAVE ON SUBLIMATION SUPPLIES

I can get you a 10% discount on Cricut supplies and materials when you order over $100 of these items from the Cricut Shop... plus free shipping in the U.S. The discount changes frequently, so to get the latest code please go to this link:

jennifermaker.com/cricutdiscount

Don't know where to start?
Check out my favorite products at
jennifermaker.com/sublimation-supplies

Recommendations for printers, paper, ink, tools, accessories, and more!

GET STARTED WITH SUBLIMATION STARTUP!

Learn how to choose and set up the sublimation printer that meets your needs, learn the tools and supplies for sublimated projects, and then learn how to design and make a fun project with Jennifer!

Find out more at
makeracademy.com/ sublimation-startup

LEARN HOW TO CREATE YOUR OWN SUBLIMATION DESIGNS WITH
CANVA CREATIVE!

Find out more at
jennifermaker.com/canva-workshop

LEARN HOW TO CREATE CUSTOM FONTS FOR YOUR SUBLIMATION PROJECTS WITH

FONTS FIRSTHAND!

Find out more at
https://jennifermaker.com/fonts-workshop

CRAFT A LIFE YOU LOVE

Visit me at JenniferMaker.com regularly for inspiration, help, and projects!

START HERE

DO YOU EVER FEEL UNINSPIRED AND STRUGGLE TO FIND UNIQUE IDEAS AND CREATIVE PROJECTS?

DO YOU WISH YOU HAD A FRIEND TO WALK YOU THROUGH A FUN PROJECT STEP BY STEP?

LOOKING FOR SOMETHING?

Search this website

WELCOME!

I inspire you to make crafts and decorate your home. I'm always working on something new and fun! Follow along on my DIY adventures, reconnect with your creativity, and read more about me here.

Welcome to JenniferMaker

Printed in Great Britain
by Amazon

56422516R00077